S0-BDK-357

The Wiersbe
BIBLE STUDY SERIES

The
Wiersbe
BIBLE STUDY SERIES

JEREMIAH

Taking

a Stand

for the

Truth

David C Cook®
transforming lives together

THE WIERSBE BIBLE STUDY SERIES: JEREMIAH
Published by David C Cook
4050 Lee Vance View
Colorado Springs, CO 80918 U.S.A.

David C Cook Distribution Canada
55 Woodslee Avenue, Paris, Ontario, Canada N3L 3E5

David C Cook U.K., Kingsway Communications
Eastbourne, East Sussex BN23 6NT, England

The graphic circle C logo is a registered trademark of David C Cook.

All rights reserved. Except for brief excerpts for review purposes,
no part of this book may be reproduced or used in any form
without written permission from the publisher.

Unless otherwise noted, all Scripture quotations in this study are taken from the Holy
Bible, New International Version®, NIV®. Copyright © 1973, 1978, 1984 by Biblica,
Inc.™ Used by permission of Zondervan. All rights reserved worldwide. www.zondervan.
com. Scripture quotations marked NASB are taken from the *New American Standard
Bible*, © Copyright 1960, 1995 by The Lockman Foundation. Used by permission.

In the *Be Decisive* excerpts, unless otherwise noted, all Scripture quotations are
taken from the King James Version of the Bible. (Public Domain.) Scripture
quotations marked NIV are taken from the Holy Bible, New International
Version®, NIV®; NKJV are taken from the New King James Version. Copyright
© 1982 by Thomas Nelson, Inc. Used by permission. All rights reserved.

All excerpts taken from *Be Decisive*, second edition, published by David C
Cook in 2010 © 1991 Warren W. Wiersbe, ISBN 978-1-4347-6634-2.

ISBN 978-1-4347-0377-4
eISBN 978-0-7814-0819-6

© 2012 Warren W. Wiersbe

The Team: Steve Parolini, Karen Lee-Thorp, Amy Konyndyk,
Sarah Schultz, Nick Lee, Jack Campbell, Karen Athen
Series Cover Design: John Hamilton Design
Cover Photo: Veer

Printed in the United States of America
First Edition 2012

1 2 3 4 5 6 7 8 9 10

121211

Contents

Introduction to Jeremiah

God's Story

"Power tends to corrupt and absolute power corrupts absolutely." Lord John Acton wrote that in a letter to his friend Mandell Creighton in April 1887. When he ended the letter, the British historian added this postscript: "History provides neither compensation for suffering nor penalties for wrong."

As you study the prophecy of Jeremiah, you'll learn that Lord Acton was right in his first statement, for you will meet in this book some of history's most powerful and corrupt rulers. But Lord Acton was terribly wrong in his postscript. God is still on the throne, and history is His story.

Decisive Leadership

Though at first Jeremiah hesitated when God called him, he surrendered to the Lord and became one of history's most decisive spiritual leaders. Tragically, however, the people who most needed his leadership rejected him and turned their backs on God's Word.

As never before, our homes, churches, cities, and nations need decisive leaders who will obey the Word of God. "If you ever injected truth into politics," quipped Will Rogers, "you have no politics." The politician asks, "Is it popular?" The diplomat asks, "Is it safe?" But the true leader asks, "Is it God's will? Is it right?" To quote James Russell Lowell's "The Present Crisis": "Truth forever on the scaffold, wrong forever on the throne, yet that scaffold sways the future, and, behind the dim unknown, standeth God within the shadow, keeping watch above His own."

That's what the Lord told Jeremiah: "I am watching over My word to perform it" (Jer. 1:12 NASB).

—*Warren W. Wiersbe*

How to Use This Study

This study is designed for both individual and small-group use. We've divided it into eight lessons—each references one or more chapters in Warren W. Wiersbe's commentary *Be Decisive* (second edition, David C Cook, 2010). While reading *Be Decisive* is not a prerequisite for going through this study, the additional insights and background Wiersbe offers can greatly enhance your study experience.

The **Getting Started** questions at the beginning of each lesson offer you an opportunity to record your first thoughts and reactions to the study text. This is an important step in the study process as those "first impressions" often include clues about what it is your heart is longing to discover.

The bulk of the study is found in the **Going Deeper** questions. These dive into the Bible text and, along with helpful excerpts from Wiersbe's commentary, help you examine not only the original context and meaning of the verses but also modern application.

Looking Inward narrows the focus down to your personal story. These intimate questions can be a bit uncomfortable at times, but don't shy away from honesty here. This is where you are asked to stand before the mirror of God's Word and look closely at what you see. It's the place to take a good look at yourself in light of the lesson and search for ways in which you can grow in faith.

Going Forward is the place where you can commit to paper those things you want or need to do in order to better live out the discoveries you made in the Looking Inward section. Don't skip or skim through this. Take the time to really consider what practical steps you might take to move closer to Christ. Then share your thoughts with a trusted friend who can act as an encourager and accountability partner.

Finally, there is a brief **Seeking Help** section to close the lesson. This is a reminder for you to invite God into your spiritual-growth process. If you choose to write out a prayer in this section, come back to it as you work through the lesson and continue to seek the Holy Spirit's guidance as you discover God's will for your life.

Tips for Small Groups

A small group is a dynamic thing. One week it might seem like a group of close-knit friends. The next it might seem more like a group of uncomfortable strangers. A small-group leader's role is to read these subtle changes and adjust the tone of the discussion accordingly.

Small groups need to be safe places for people to talk openly. It is through shared wrestling with difficult life issues that some of the greatest personal growth is discovered. But in order for the group to feel safe, participants need to know it's okay *not* to share sometimes. Always invite honest disclosure, but never force someone to speak if he or she isn't comfortable doing so. (A savvy leader will follow up later with a group member who isn't comfortable sharing in a group setting to see if a one-on-one discussion is more appropriate.)

Have volunteers take turns reading excerpts from Scripture or from the commentary. The more each person is involved even in the mundane tasks, the more they'll feel comfortable opening up in more meaningful ways.

The leader should watch the clock and keep the discussion moving. Sometimes there may be more Going Deeper questions than your group can cover in your available time. If you've had a fruitful discussion, it's okay to move on without finishing everything. And if you think the group is getting bogged down on a question or has taken off on a tangent, you can simply say, "Let's go on to question 5." Be sure to save at least ten to fifteen minutes for the Going Forward questions.

Finally, soak your group meetings in prayer—before you begin, during as needed, and always at the end of your time together.

Reluctance
(JEREMIAH 1)

Before you begin …
- *Pray for the Holy Spirit to reveal truth and wisdom as you go through this lesson.*
- *Read Jeremiah 1. This lesson references chapter 1 in* Be Decisive. *It will be helpful for you to have your Bible and a copy of the commentary available as you work through this lesson.*

Getting Started

From the Commentary

Jeremiah's father Hilkiah was a priest as was his father before him, and young Jeremiah was also expected to serve at the altar. He may even have been at the age when he would have stepped into his place of ministry when God called him to be a prophet.

Since serving as a prophet was much more demanding than serving as a priest, it's no wonder Jeremiah demurred.

If I had my choice, I'd take the priesthood! For one thing, a priest's duties were predictable. Just about everything he had to do was written down in the law. Thus, all the priest had to do was follow instructions. Day after day, there were sacrifices to offer, lepers to examine, unclean people to exclude from the camp, cleansed people to reinstate, official ceremonies to observe, a sanctuary to care for, and the law to teach. No wonder some of the priests said, "Oh, what a weariness!" (Mal. 1:13 NKJV).

—*Be Decisive*, pages 15–16

1. What made the ministry of a prophet so challenging? How did Jeremiah respond to his call to be a prophet? How did God change his mind?

More to Consider: The word heart *is used at least sixty-six times in the book of Jeremiah. What does this tell us about Jeremiah? About God's choice of Jeremiah to be a prophet?*

2. Choose one verse or phrase from Jeremiah 1 that stands out to you. This could be something you're intrigued by, something that makes you

uncomfortable, something that puzzles you, something that resonates with you, or just something you want to examine further. Write that here.

Going Deeper

From the Commentary

In his ministry, Jeremiah had to be

• a destroyer and a builder (1:9–10)

• a pillar and a wall (1:17–18)

• a watchman (6:17)

• a tester of metals (6:27–30)

• a physician (8:11, 21–22)

• a sacrificial lamb (11:19)

• a long-distance runner (12:5)

• a shepherd (13:17, 20; 17:16 NIV)

• a troublemaker (15:10, 15–17)

—*Be Decisive*, page 17

3. As you learn about Jeremiah in the first chapter, what stands out to you about his character? About the roles God had given him? Skim the verses listed above to get an overview of Jeremiah's various roles. In what ways does a prophet's job involve each of these roles?

From the Commentary

Jeremiah was born during the reign of King Manasseh, the most evil man who ever reigned over the kingdom of Judah (2 Kings 21:1–18). The son of godly Hezekiah, Manasseh came to the throne when only twelve years old, and the officials around him easily influenced him toward idolatry. "Manasseh seduced them [the people of Judah] to do more evil than the nations whom the Lord had destroyed before the children of Israel" (v. 9 NKJV). When Manasseh died, his evil son Amon continued his father's evil practices.

Thus, Jeremiah grew up in Anathoth at a time when idolatry flourished in Judah, children were offered in sacrifice to idols, the law of Moses was disregarded and disobeyed, and it looked as though there was no hope for the nation. Godly priests were not greatly appreciated.

—*Be Decisive*, pages 17–18

4. How did the culture of the time (flourishing idolatry) determine when God chose to raise up a prophet? Why was idolatry such a dangerous practice? How might the prospect of speaking out against common practices, however evil, have influenced Jeremiah's initial response to God's call? Could he have rejected the call from God? Why or why not?

From Today's World

It's easy for political leaders to invite religious leaders in for consultation and then do exactly what they'd already planned to do. Today, it's good public relations to give people the impression that religion is important. Consider the role religion plays in politics—especially during election campaigns. Nearly all politicians ally themselves with one particular belief system or another—and in most cases in the United States that belief system is Christianity.

5. What role does religion play in the leadership of your country? What role (if any) should it play? What is the proper role of religious advisers in government? How was Jeremiah's role similar to and different from the religious advisers of our time?

From the Commentary

> Jeremiah preached to the nation for forty years, giv-
> ing them God's promises and warnings; yet he lived
> to see Jerusalem and his beloved temple destroyed by
> Nebuchadnezzar's army and his people taken captive to
> Babylon. Jeremiah ministered in turbulent times and
> yet remained faithful to the Lord. He exposed the futile
> foreign policy of the rulers, pleading with them to turn
> to the Lord with all their hearts and trust God instead of
> trusting their political allies. Jeremiah is one of Scripture's
> greatest examples of faithfulness and decisive action in
> the face of physical danger and national decay.
>
> —*Be Decisive*, pages 19–20

6. Given the fact that God's people were taken into captivity, was Jeremiah's
prophetic life a failure? Explain. How can you know if a prophet has been
"successful"? What role, ultimately, did Jeremiah play in God's unfolding
story?

From the Commentary

Jeremiah hesitated as he looked at the work before him and the wickedness around him, and when he looked at the weakness within himself, Jeremiah was certain that he wasn't the man for the job.

When it comes to serving the Lord, there's a sense in which nobody is adequate. "And who is sufficient for these things?" (2 Cor. 2:16) asked the great apostle Paul as he pondered the responsibilities of ministry. Paul then answered his own question: "Not that we are sufficient of ourselves to think any thing as of ourselves; but our sufficiency is of God" (3:5).

—*Be Decisive*, page 20

7. What's the difference between knowing our weaknesses and saying that our weaknesses prevent God from accomplishing anything through us? How is this like the dilemma Jeremiah faced? In this initial exchange, what did God know that Jeremiah didn't know?

From the Commentary

> A prophet was a chosen and authorized spokesman for
> God who declared God's Word to the people. The Hebrew
> word probably comes from an Arabic root that means
> "to announce." For example, Moses spoke to Aaron, and
> Aaron was his spokesman (prophet) before Pharaoh (Ex.
> 7:1–2). Prophets did more than reveal the future, for their
> messages had present application to the life of the nation.
> They were *forth*tellers more than *fore*tellers, exposing the
> sins of the people and calling them back to their covenant
> responsibilities before God.
>
> —*Be Decisive,* page 21

8. In what ways did Jeremiah's messages have application for his audience's
present circumstances? What were some of the things Jeremiah revealed
to the people in his prophecy? How did God intend to use these truths to
bring the people back to Himself?

More to Consider: Review Jeremiah 1:5. What makes each of the phrases in this verse important?

From the Commentary

Jeremiah's ministry was difficult because he had to tear down before he could build, and he had to root up before he could plant. In too many ministries, there are organizational "structures" that don't belong there and should be torn down because they're hindering progress. Some "plants" are taking up space but bearing no fruit, and they ought to be pulled up. Jesus said, "Every plant which My heavenly Father has not planted will be uprooted" (Matt. 15:13 NKJV).

Any servant of God who feels himself or herself too weak to serve needs to consider these three encouragements. Has God called you? Then He will equip you and enable you. Are you obeying His commands by faith? Then He is with you to protect you. Are you sharing the Word? Then He will accomplish His purposes no matter how the people respond. Jeremiah's name means "Jehovah establishes," and God did establish His servant and his ministry and cared for him to the very end. "But the Lord is faithful, who will establish you and guard you from the evil one" (2 Thess. 3:3 NKJV).

—*Be Decisive*, page 23

9. What were some of the things Jeremiah had to "root up" before he could build? How are these similar to the challenges faced in the church today?

From the Commentary

> When you study the Old Testament prophets, you discover that three strands of truth wove their messages together: (1) *past sin:* the nation has disobeyed God's law; (2) *present responsibility:* the people must repent or God will send judgment; and (3) *future hope:* the Lord will come one day and establish His glorious kingdom.
>
> The Lord didn't give Jeremiah a joyful message of deliverance to announce, but rather a tragic message of judgment. So dangerous was this message that people hearing it called Jeremiah a traitor. He would be misunderstood, persecuted, arrested, and imprisoned—and more than once, his life was in danger. The nation didn't want to hear the truth, but Jeremiah told them plainly that they were defying the Lord, disobeying the law, and destined for judgment.

God gave Jeremiah three promises to prepare him f
dangerous mission.

—*Be Decisive*, pages 23–24

10. Review Jeremiah 1:11–19. In what ways was Jeremiah's mission dangerous? What promises did God give Jeremiah to prepare him for this dangerous mission?

Looking Inward

Take a moment to reflect on all that you've explored thus far in this study of Jeremiah 1. Review your notes and answers and think about how each of these things matters in your life today.

Tips for Small Groups: To get the most out of this section, form pairs or trios and have group members take turns answering these questions. Be honest and as open as you can in this discussion, but most of all, be encouraging and supportive of others. Be sensitive to those who are going through particularly difficult times and don't press for people to speak if they're uncomfortable doing so.

11. Jeremiah had some initial reluctance when God called him to be a prophet. What are some examples of your own reluctance toward God? What is at the root of your reluctance? How can you overcome this reluctance? How have you done so in the past?

12. Jeremiah had to say hard truths to an unreceptive audience. Have you ever had to do this? If so, describe the circumstances. What made this a difficult situation? What helped you through it? What did it teach you about God's presence? About yourself?

13. When have you had to trust God's leading like Jeremiah? What makes trusting God difficult? Why is it essential for all who choose to follow God?

Going Forward

14. Think of one or two things that you have learned that you'd like to work on in the coming week. Remember that this is all about quality, not quantity. It's better to work on one specific area of life and do it well than to work on many and do poorly (or to be so overwhelmed that you simply don't try).

Do you want to be more receptive to God's call? Do you want to learn more about what He's calling you to do? Be specific. Go back through Jeremiah 1 and put a star next to the phrase or verse that is most encouraging to you. Consider memorizing this verse.

Real-Life Application Ideas: Jeremiah's message was multifaceted, but the primary focus was encouraging God's people to turn away from evil and ungodly practices and turn back toward God. Consider any activities or behaviors that tend to turn you away from God—your "idols," so to speak. Why do you keep hanging onto these activities or behaviors? Think of practical ways to turn away from them and back toward God. It might be helpful to talk with a trusted friend about the specifics so you can be held accountable.

Seeking Help

15. Write a prayer below (or simply pray one in silence), inviting God to work on your mind and heart in those areas you've noted in the Going Forward section. Be honest about your desires and fears.

Notes for Small Groups:

- *Look for ways to put into practice the things you wrote in the Going Forward section. Talk with other group members about your ideas and commit to being accountable to one another.*

- *During the coming week, ask the Holy Spirit to continue to reveal truth to you from what you've read and studied.*

- *Before you start the next lesson, read Jeremiah 2—6. For more in-depth lesson preparation, read chapter 2, "The Prophet Preaches," in* Be Decisive.

The Preaching Prophet
(JEREMIAH 2—6)

Before you begin …
- *Pray for the Holy Spirit to reveal truth and wisdom as you go through this lesson.*
- *Read Jeremiah 2—6. This lesson references chapter 2 in* Be Decisive. *It will be helpful for you to have your Bible and a copy of the commentary available as you work through this lesson.*

Getting Started

From the Commentary

In my library is a notebook containing the outlines of messages that I preached when I began my ministry back in 1950. Whenever I read those outlines, I feel very embarrassed and contrite in heart, and I marvel that anybody ever listened to those sermons or came back to hear more. A seasoned preacher once said, "When you're young in the ministry, you can't understand why more people don't come to hear you. But when you get older, you're amazed that anybody comes to hear you." I agree.

Young Jeremiah, however, started his ministry with messages that were courageous, compassionate, and convicting. Boldly he confronted the people with their sins and pled with them to repent and return to the Lord. Four major themes combine in these messages: rebellion, repentance, righteousness, and retribution.

—*Be Decisive*, page 31

1. Why is it significant that Jeremiah is described as a young man? How might this have affected the manner in which his message was delivered? Received? What does God's decision to use a young man for such a big, important task teach us about God?

2. Choose one verse or phrase from Jeremiah 2—6 that stands out to you. This could be something you're intrigued by, something that makes you uncomfortable, something that puzzles you, something that resonates with you, or just something you want to examine further. Write that here.

Going Deeper

From the Commentary

When the Lord gave the Israelites His covenant at Mount Sinai (Ex. 19—20), He entered into a loving relationship with them that He compared to marriage. "They broke my covenant, though I was a husband to them" (Jer. 31:32 NIV; see 3:14). In the Old Testament, Israel's idolatry is compared to adultery and even prostitution (see Isa. 54:5; Hos. 2:19). At the beginning of this covenant relationship, the Jews were devoted to the Lord and loved Him, but once they conquered the Promised Land, their hearts lusted after the gods of the nations around them and they sank into idolatry (Judg. 1—3). Although God had taken them safely through their wilderness journey and given them a wonderful inheritance in Canaan, they abandoned Him for man-made gods. What kind of loyal love is that?

—Be Decisive, page 32

3. Review Jeremiah 2:1–8. Why do you think God used the marriage comparison when talking about Israel? How is this comparison used in other parts of the Bible? Why is it such an apt illustration? What does it reveal about God's message about marriage?

From the Commentary

A basic principle is enunciated in Jeremiah 2:19: God punishes us by allowing our own sins to bring pain and discipline to our lives. "Your own conduct and actions have brought this upon you. This is your punishment. How bitter it is!" (4:18 NIV). "Your wrongdoings have kept these [rains] away; your sins have deprived you of good" (5:25 NIV). The greatest judgment God can send to disobedient people is to let them have their own way and reap the sad, painful consequences of their sins.

—*Be Decisive*, page 33

4. In what ways was the nation backsliding? Respond to this statement: "The greatest judgment God can send to disobedient people is to let them have their own way and reap the sad, painful consequences of their sins." How was this true in the book of Jeremiah? What evidence do we have that this is still true today?

More to Consider: Jeremiah often used animals to describe the behavior of people, and in Jeremiah 2:20, he compared the Jews to an unruly animal that would not wear the yoke. One of his recurring themes is the stubbornness of their evil hearts. Review the following examples: Jeremiah 3:17; 7:24; 9:14; 11:8; 13:10; 16:12; 18:12; 23:17. Why is this theme hammered home so much? Read Psalm 32:9; Proverbs 7:21–23; and Hosea 4:16. What do these verses tell us about people who refuse to obey God?

From the Commentary

God chastened the wayward Israelites many times for their sins, but they refused to change their ways, and then they even blamed God! He brought charges against them (Jer. 2:9 NKJV), but instead of confessing and repenting, they complained and brought charges against Him! None of His discipline seemed to do any good. "You struck them, but they felt no pain; you crushed them, but they refused correction" (5:3 NIV; see 7:28; 17:23; 32:33; 35:13).

God reminded the people how richly He had blessed them. Yet they rebelled against Him (2:29), forgot Him (v. 32), and lied to Him (vv. 33–35), claiming to be innocent. One of the major themes of the book of Deuteronomy is that the nation should remember the Lord and what He had done for them. Yet the people took their blessings for granted and gave their allegiance to dumb idols. They were so skilled at their harlotry, worshipping false gods, that even the most wicked prostitute could learn new things from them! They exploited the poor and were stained by their blood, and yet they pleaded innocence (see Amos 2:6–8; 5:10–12).

—*Be Decisive*, page 35

5. Why did the backslidden followers try to turn the judgment against them back toward God? Why did they try to deflect blame? What did they claim as proof of their innocence? Read Psalms 37 and 73 and Matthew 5:45. What do these passages reveal about the relationship between prosperity and God's blessing? What should God's goodness have led the people toward? (See Luke 15:17–18; Rom. 2:4–5.)

From the Commentary

In Jeremiah 3:1—4:4 the prophet used four vivid images to picture the sad spiritual condition of the kingdom of Judah.

Here are the first two:

The unfaithful wife (3:1–10). Jeremiah returned to the metaphor of marriage that he had used in 2:1–2, but this time he introduced the subject of divorce. The Mosaic law permitted a man to divorce his wife, but it did not allow him to marry her again (Deut. 24:1–4). God had every right to reject His people, because they had abandoned Him, not in order to marry another "husband," but in order to play the harlot with *many* lovers. The people had gone to the hills and built shrines dedicated to foreign gods. They had acted worse than common prostitutes, who at least waited for lovers to come to them, for Judah had *pursued* false gods and repeatedly committed spiritual adultery with them.

The unhealthy patient (3:21–25). In Scripture, sickness is one of many metaphors for sin (Ps. 41:4; Isa. 1:5–6; Jer. 8:22; 30:12; Mark 2:17). Like an infection entering the bloodstream, sin secretly gets into the system of the "inner man" and goes to work weakening and destroying. It gradually infects the whole system, producing spiritual lassitude and loss of spiritual appetite; and if not cared for, the "sin sickness" can lead to dire consequences. When we hear about believers suddenly falling into open sin, in most cases a gradual slide preceded the sudden fall.

—Be Decisive, pages 36–37

6. How might the people who were already distancing themselves from God have reacted to these metaphors? How does each of these two images reveal the heart of God? The sins of the people?

From the Commentary

Here are the second two images:

The unplowed field (4:1–3). The problem with the people was their dishonesty; they would use the right language, but they wouldn't mean it from their hearts. They would pray to the true God, but not forsake the false gods. It was easy to say, "As the Lord lives," but they didn't say it in truth, justice, and righteousness. Their hearts were hard and crowded with thorns like a neglected, unplowed field.

The uncircumcised heart (4:4). Jewish boys were circumcised when eight days old, given a name, and made a son of the covenant (Gen. 17:9–14; Lev. 12:3; Luke 1:59). Although no amount of surgery on the body could change the heart, the Jews thought that this ritual was their guarantee of salvation (Matt. 3:7–9; Acts 15:1–5). God, however, wanted them to "operate" on their hearts and put away their callousness and disobedience. "Therefore circumcise the foreskin of your heart, and be stiff-necked no longer" (Deut. 10:16 NKJV; see also 30:6).

—*Be Decisive*, page 38

7. Read Hosea 10:12 and Matthew 13:1–9, 18–23. How are these passages similar to what Jeremiah says about the unplowed fields? Read Romans 2:28–29 and Colossians 2:11. What do these verses say in support of the "circumcision of the heart"? What does Jeremiah 6:10 add to this teaching?

From the Commentary

> The Lord even called to the dispersed Israelites to return
> to Him. This invitation reminds us of God's promises
> in Leviticus 26:40–45, Deuteronomy 30, and 1 Kings
> 8:46–53, which assured them that God would forgive if
> they would repent. In Jeremiah 3:14–19, Jeremiah seemed
> to be looking far ahead to the kingdom age when Israel
> and Judah would be united, the nation would be purified
> and multiplied, and God would give them spiritual lead-
> ers to care for them. In the darkest days of their history,
> the Israelites heard their prophets announce this coming
> messianic kingdom, and the promise gave them hope.
>
> —*Be Decisive*, page 39

8. Review Jeremiah 4:11–18. What judgments did God pronounce on
Israel? Why? What was Jeremiah's response to these judgments (see v. 19)?
What do we discover about God's character from this passage?

More to Consider: Jeremiah is known as the weeping prophet. In 4:19–31, he expressed his personal anguish. (See also 6:24; 9:10; 10:19–20.) What does this tell us about Jeremiah's heart?

From the Commentary

Since the people would not listen to God's word, God told Jeremiah to act out His message. Chapter 5 includes the first of at least ten "action sermons" found in Jeremiah. This chapter deals with four sins of the people of Jerusalem.

They were ungodly (vv. 1–6).

They were ungrateful (vv. 7–9).

They were unfaithful (vv. 10–19).

They were unconcerned (vv. 20–31).

—*Be Decisive*, pages 41–43

9. Read the associated passage and consider each of the sins listed above. In what ways did Jeremiah's audience commit each of these sins? Does the church deal with the same sins today? Explain. What might a modern-day Jeremiah say to us about those sins?

From the Commentary

> The closing section of Jeremiah's sermon in chapter 6 focuses on the invading Babylonian army and the devastation they will bring to the kingdom of Judah. In that critical hour, the prophet told the nation what God was doing.
>
> Sometimes suffering brings out the best in people, but that wouldn't happen in the siege of Jerusalem. When God turned on the furnace, it would reveal the people as rejected silver, nothing but dross to be thrown away. He wasn't purifying them; He was punishing them. They weren't being refined; they were being rejected. They were too cheap to preserve.
>
> —*Be Decisive*, pages 44–45

10. Review Jeremiah 6. What is God's message in this chapter? What are the "ancient paths" referred to in verse 16? What is the crossroads? What does it mean to "ask … where the good way is, and walk in it"?

Looking Inward

Take a moment to reflect on all that you've explored thus far in this study of Jeremiah 2—6. Review your notes and answers and think about how each of these things matters in your life today.

Tips for Small Groups: To get the most out of this section, form pairs or trios and have group members take turns answering these questions. Be honest and as open as you can in this discussion, but most of all, be encouraging and supportive of others. Be sensitive to those who are going through particularly difficult times and don't press for people to speak if they're uncomfortable doing so.

11. Jeremiah was a young man doing important work for God. What are some of the challenging things God asked you to do when you were young (either in calendar years or spiritual "age")? What obstacles did you face because of your youth? How did God help you accomplish His purposes?

12. The nation of Israel was backsliding. Have you ever backslidden? If so, what led to your movement away from God? How did you discover you were heading in the wrong direction? What did you do to turn back and follow God again?

13. God promised punishment to the people if they didn't repent. Does God punish believers today for their sins? Explain. Have you ever felt like God was punishing you for sinning? If so, what made you feel that way? If it wasn't truly punishment from God, what might God have been doing when you thought He was punishing you?

Going Forward

14. Think of one or two things that you have learned that you'd like to work on in the coming week. Remember that this is all about quality, not quantity. It's better to work on one specific area of life and do it well than to work on many and do poorly (or to be so overwhelmed that you simply don't try).

Do you want to repent of something? Do you want to overcome reluctance to follow God's call? Be specific. Go back through Jeremiah 2—6 and put a star next to the phrase or verse that is most encouraging to you. Consider memorizing this verse.

Real-Life Application Ideas: One of the messages in Jeremiah is that God can use anyone—no matter what age or situation in life—to do great things (and difficult things). Take inventory of the things God is asking you to do today. Perhaps He's asking you to speak to friends or family members or even strangers about your faith. Maybe He wants you to volunteer at church or elsewhere in your community. What would it take for you to trust God and do what He's asking of you? Work on those things in this coming week.

Seeking Help

15. Write a prayer below (or simply pray one in silence), inviting God to work on your mind and heart in those areas you've noted in the Going Forward section. Be honest about your desires and fears.

Notes for Small Groups:

- *Look for ways to put into practice the things you wrote in the Going Forward section. Talk with other group members about your ideas and commit to being accountable to one another.*

- *During the coming week, ask the Holy Spirit to continue to reveal truth to you from what you've read and studied.*

- *Before you start the next lesson, read Jeremiah 7—13. For more in-depth lesson preparation, read chapters 3 and 4, "The Voice in the Temple" and "Voting with God," in* Be Decisive.

The Temple Voice
(JEREMIAH 7—13)

Before you begin …
- *Pray for the Holy Spirit to reveal truth and wisdom as you go through this lesson.*
- *Read Jeremiah 7—13. This lesson references chapters 3 and 4 in* Be Decisive. *It will be helpful for you to have your Bible and a copy of the commentary available as you work through this lesson.*

Getting Started

From the Commentary

The Jews knew that idolatry was wrong, but they were confident they had nothing to fear. After all, God would *never* permit anything terrible to happen to the city where His holy temple was located! Didn't Judah possess the law of Moses, and weren't the Jews the children of Abraham and the sons of the covenant? They were God's chosen people! With a religious heritage like that, no evil could ever fall on their kingdom!

God, however, had quite a different view of the matter. He commanded Jeremiah to go up to the temple and proclaim His message to the hypocritical people gathered there. In this courageous sermon, the prophet exposed the nation's *false worship* (Jer. 7:1—8:3), their *false prophets* (8:4–22), their *false confidence* in the covenant they were disobeying (9:1–26), and the *false gods* they were worshipping (10:1–25). In other words, Jeremiah dealt with their sinful mistreatment of the temple, the law, the covenant, and the Lord Himself. It wasn't a popular message to deliver, and it almost cost him his life!

—Be Decisive, pages 50–51

1. What must it have been like for Jeremiah to go right into the heart of the conflict to speak to God's people? Why did God send him there instead of have him speak in a more neutral site? What does this say about God's disappointment in His chosen people? About Jeremiah's trust in God?

2. Choose one verse or phrase from Jeremiah 7—13 that stands out to you. This could be something you're intrigued by, something that makes you uncomfortable, something that puzzles you, something that resonates with you, or just something you want to examine further. Write that here.

Going Deeper

From the Commentary

> Three times a year, the Jewish men were required to go up
> to the temple in Jerusalem to celebrate the feasts (Deut.
> 16:16), and this may have been one of those occasions.
> The temple was probably crowded, but there weren't
> many true worshippers there. The prophet stood at one
> of the gates that led into the temple courts, and there he
> preached to the people as they came in. He presented
> God's four indictments against the people of Judah.
>
> —*Be Decisive*, page 51

3. What were the four indictments Jeremiah preached against the people
at the temple? (See Jer. 7:1–15, 16–20, 21–26; 7:27—8:3.) What was God's
promise if they changed their ways?

*More to Consider: Read Matthew 21:13. How do Jesus' words relate
to Jeremiah's message? (See Jer. 7:11.) Note: A "den of robbers" is the
place where thieves go to hide after they've committed their crimes.*

From the Commentary

Having shattered the popular illusions about the temple, Jeremiah then exposed the false prophets who constantly opposed his ministry and led the people astray. He raised a number of questions in this section, but the whole proclamation centers on one major question: "Why did the nation not turn back to God?" In answering the question, Jeremiah dealt with three aspects of the people's stubborn refusal to obey God.

Their refusal was irrational (Jer. 8:4–7). Jeremiah used analogies from human life and nature to illustrate his point. When people fall down, they get up again. That's the sensible thing to do. If they find themselves walking on the wrong path, they retrace their steps and get on the right path. Conclusion: If people can be sensible about these everyday matters, why can't they be sensible about eternal matters, especially since the consequences are much more tragic?

Their refusal was caused by deception (Jer. 8:8–12). "Lo, they have rejected the word of the Lord; and what wisdom is in them?" (Jer. 8:9). Just as they boasted that they possessed the temple, so they boasted that they had the divine law (v. 8), *but possessing the Scriptures isn't the same as practicing the Scriptures*. Although the Bible is still a best seller, its popularity isn't keeping Western society from crumbling morally and spiritually. There appears to be no connection between what people say they believe and the way people act.

Their refusal would lead to judgment (Jer. 8:13–22). These

verses blend three voices: God's voice of judgment, the people's voice of despair, and the prophet's voice of anguish as he contemplated the ruin of a once-great nation. God declared that the fields would be ruined (v. 13), the cities would be destroyed (v. 17), and the people would be either slain or taken captive (v. 19). It would be like drinking poison (8:14; 9:15; 23:15), experiencing an earthquake (8:16), being attacked by venomous snakes (v. 17), or being crushed and broken (v. 21).

—*Be Decisive*, pages 55–56

4. Review Jeremiah 8:4–22. Why were the Jews so stubborn to obey God? What tempted them away from God in the first place? What tempts believers away from faith today? How is this similar to what the Jews in Jeremiah's time struggled with?

From the Commentary

The Jews are the only nation in history with whom God has entered into a covenant relationship (Gen. 12:1–3). As the children of Abraham, marked by the seal of circumcision (Gen. 17), they are indeed a special people to the Lord (Ex. 19:4–6). The tragedy is that they trusted the covenant and the ritual to guarantee them acceptance before the Lord. They thought they didn't need to repent or believe; that was for the uncircumcised Gentiles.

—Be Decisive, page 57

5. Review Jeremiah 9. Why did the Jews trust the covenant as some sort of "get out of trouble free" card? How did John the Baptist face something similar in his ministry (Matt. 3:7–10)? How did Jesus deal with this (John 8:33–47)?

From the Commentary

Before Abraham trusted in the true God, he had been a worshipper of idols (Josh. 24:2–3). During their years in Egypt, the Jews were exposed to the gross idolatry of that land, and some of it stayed in their hearts. While Moses was meeting with God on Mount Sinai, the people, aided by Moses' brother Aaron, made a golden calf and worshipped it (Ex. 32). At Sinai, they had seen the glory of God, heard the voice of God, and accepted the law of God; yet "they changed their glory into the image of an ox that eats grass" (Ps. 106:20 NKJV). Idolatry was in their hearts.

—*Be Decisive*, pages 59–60

6. Review Jeremiah 10. Why was idolatry so prevalent in Old Testament times? How did it continue into Jesus' day? What are the popular idols in today's world? What causes people to create and follow idols?

From the Commentary

In his poem "The Need of the Hour," the American poet Edwin Markham wrote, "We need the faith to go a path untrod, / The power to be alone and vote with God." That's what Jeremiah was doing during the reign of King Josiah—he was walking alone and voting with God. King Josiah was excited when the workmen repairing the temple found the book of the law (2 Kings 22), and this discovery led to a movement that temporarily cleansed the kingdom of idolatry (2 Kings 23). This event is commonly called "Josiah's revival," but "reformation" might be a more accurate word. Why? Because the people obeyed the law only outwardly; in their hearts they still held on to their idols.

Because Jeremiah understood this and knew the shallowness of the unrepentant human heart, he wasn't too vocal during Josiah's reformation. He knew what the people were doing in secret and that they would return to their sins at the first opportunity. In this section of his prophecy, Jeremiah recorded the sins of the nation and pleaded with the people to return to the Lord while there was yet time.

—*Be Decisive*, pages 65–66

7. How did the people hold idolatry in their hearts? What did Jeremiah say to turn the people's hearts? In what ways was Jeremiah's own response to God (Jer. 11:5) an example for the way Israel was supposed to respond to God's covenant (see Deut. 27:9–26; Josh. 8:30–35)? What would have happened if the people had changed their ways and followed God?

From the Commentary

The Lord revealed to His servant a twofold conspiracy in the land: a conspiracy of the men of Judah to disobey the covenant and resist the reforms led by King Josiah (Jer. 11:9–17), and a conspiracy of the people in Jeremiah's hometown to kill the prophet and silence God's Word (11:18—12:6). Both led to a third crisis that threatened Jeremiah's own faith in the Lord.

—*Be Decisive*, page 68

8. Review Jeremiah 11:9–17. In what ways was this conspiracy against the king actually a rebellion against God? Read 11:18–23. What prompted the conspiracy against Jeremiah? Why did the priests in Anathoth listen to the false prophets? What does this tell us about people who hold religious offices?

More to Consider: Read Jeremiah 1:7–8, 17–19. How do these verses apply to the challenges Jeremiah faced in chapter 11? How did God keep Jeremiah strong in the midst of these challenges? What can church leaders learn and apply from Jeremiah's experience?

From the Commentary

No sooner did God take care of the two conspiracies than Jeremiah found himself struggling with a theological crisis (Jer. 12:1–6). "In the commencement of the spiritual life," wrote the French mystic Madame Guyon, "our hardest task is to bear with our neighbor; in its progress, with ourselves; and in its end, with God." Jeremiah couldn't understand why a holy God would permit the false prophets and the unfaithful priests to prosper in their ministries while he, a faithful servant of God, was treated like a sacrificial lamb.

"Why does the way of the wicked prosper?" (Jer. 12:1 NIV) is a question that was asked frequently in Scripture, and it's being asked today. Job wrestled with it (Job 12; 21); the psalmists tried to understand it (Ps. 37; 49; 73); and other prophets besides Jeremiah grappled with the problem (Hab. 1; Mal. 2:17; 3:15). Jewish theologians, pointing to the covenants, taught that God blesses those who obey and judges those who disobey, but the situation in real life seemed just the opposite! How could a holy God of love allow such a thing to happen?

—Be Decisive, pages 71–72

9. How was Jeremiah's theological dilemma similar to the problem of wicked people that believers have wrestled with for ages? What answer did Jeremiah seem to want from God? Was this a crisis of faith for Jeremiah? Why or why not? How did he ultimately respond to the situation?

From the Commentary

> God used what Jeremiah said and did to speak to the people
> of Judah and warn them of the terrible judgment that was
> coming. Comfortable in their false confidence and encour-
> aged by the false prophets, the leaders and people of Judah
> were living in a fool's paradise, certain that nothing terrible
> could happen to either the Holy City or the temple.
>
> —*Be Decisive*, page 74

10. List the eight vivid images in Jeremiah 12:7—13:27 that depict the judgment that was about to fall. What did each of these images say to God's people? What does this entire episode say to us today about God's judgment?

Looking Inward

Take a moment to reflect on all that you've explored thus far in this study of Jeremiah 7—13. Review your notes and answers and think about how each of these things matters in your life today.

Tips for Small Groups: To get the most out of this section, form pairs or trios and have group members take turns answering these questions. Be honest and as open as you can in this discussion, but most of all, be encouraging and supportive of others. Be sensitive to those who are going through particularly difficult times and don't press for people to speak if they're uncomfortable doing so.

11. What are some of the idols you've wrestled with over the years? Why are you tempted by these things? What does God want to say to you about the idols you currently struggle with? What help do you need to break free of these idols?

12. God's chosen were a stubborn people at times. What are some of the ways you've been stubborn in your relationship with God? What causes that stubbornness? What are some steps you can take to overcome a tendency to be stubborn toward God?

13. Jeremiah's theological dilemma didn't stop him from following God, but it did give him pause to consider what God was up to. What are some of the questions about God that puzzle or trouble you? How do you deal with not knowing what God is up to?

Going Forward

14. Think of one or two things that you have learned that you'd like to work on in the coming week. Remember that this is all about quality, not quantity. It's better to work on one specific area of life and do it well than to work on many and do poorly (or to be so overwhelmed that you simply don't try).

Do you need to work on your stubbornness? Give up an idol? Be specific. Go back through Jeremiah 7—13 and put a star next to the phrase or verse that is most encouraging to you. Consider memorizing this verse.

Real-Life Application Ideas: Take a look at the things in your life that are possible idols, things that take you away from God instead of move you closer to Him. This could be anything from sports to food to Internet addiction. (You might want to talk with a close friend if you're not sure what your possible idols are.) Then make a plan to give up those idols and stick to it.

Seeking Help

15. Write a prayer below (or simply pray one in silence), inviting God to work on your mind and heart in those areas you've noted in the Going Forward section. Be honest about your desires and fears.

Notes for Small Groups:
- *Look for ways to put into practice the things you wrote in the Going Forward section. Talk with other group members about your ideas and commit to being accountable to one another.*
- *During the coming week, ask the Holy Spirit to continue to reveal truth to you from what you've read and studied.*
- *Before you start the next lesson, read Jeremiah 14—20. For more in-depth lesson preparation, read chapters 5 and 6, "Sermons, Supplications, and Sobs" and "The Prophet, the Potter, and the Policeman," in* Be Decisive.

Prophet and Policeman

(JEREMIAH 14—20)

Before you begin …

- *Pray for the Holy Spirit to reveal truth and wisdom as you go through this lesson.*
- *Read Jeremiah 14—20. This lesson references chapters 5 and 6 in* Be Decisive. *It will be helpful for you to have your Bible and a copy of the commentary available as you work through this lesson.*

Getting Started

From the Commentary

In Jeremiah 14—17, the prophet delivered four messages, and interspersed with these messages are his own prayers to the Lord and the answers he received. Jeremiah was bold before men but broken before God, and yet it was his brokenness that gave him his strength.

His first message was about the drought (Jer. 14:1–22). Unlike the land of Egypt, whose food supply depended on irrigation from the Nile River, the land of Canaan depended on the rains God sent from heaven (Deut. 11:10–12). If His people obeyed His law, God would send the rains and give them bumper crops (Lev. 26:3–5), but if they disobeyed, the heavens would become like iron and the earth like bronze (Lev. 26:18–20; Deut. 11:13–17; 28:22–24). Over the years, Judah's sins had brought a series of droughts to the land (see Jer. 3:3; 5:24; 12:4; 23:10), and Jeremiah used this painful but timely topic as the basis for a sermon to the people.

—*Be Decisive*, pages 81–82

1. Why was drought such a devastating thing to God's people? What does it say about the seriousness of their sins that God chose to speak about droughts through Jeremiah?

More to Consider: "Rend your heart and not your garments" (Joel 2:13) was the prophet Joel's counsel to the Jews during another time of great calamity. And David, when he sought God's forgiveness, said, "The sacrifices of God are a broken spirit; a broken and a contrite heart, O God, you will not despise" (Ps. 51:17).

2. Choose one verse or phrase from Jeremiah 14—20 that stands out to you. This could be something you're intrigued by, something that makes you uncomfortable, something that puzzles you, something that resonates with you, or just something you want to examine further. Write that here.

Going Deeper

From the Commentary

Jeremiah's second message was a prophecy about the coming captivity (Jer. 15:1–21).

Before the Jews even entered the Promised Land, Moses had rehearsed with them the terms of the covenant, warning them that God would remove them from the land if they refused to obey His voice (Deut. 28:63–68). No sooner did Joshua and that generation of spiritual leaders pass from the scene (Judg. 2:7–15) than the nation turned to idolatry and God had to chasten them. First, He punished them *in the land* by allowing other nations to invade and take control. Then, when the people cried out for help, He raised up deliverers (vv. 16–23). By the time of Jeremiah, however, the sins of the people were so great that God had to remove them *from the land* and punish them in distant Babylon.

—Be Decisive, page 85

3. Why should Jeremiah's prophecy about captivity have gotten the people's attention? How important was "place" to the Jews? Why? How would you explain in your own words God's response to Jeremiah's prayer? (See Jer. 15:1–9.) What was Jeremiah's response to God's answer? (See vv. 10–21.)

From the Commentary

The third message was about Jeremiah's strange conduct (Jer. 16:1–21).

In order to get the attention of the people, God sometimes told the prophets to do unusual things. Isaiah gave two of

his sons odd names, which he used as a text for a message
(Isa. 8), and he also dressed like a prisoner of war to call
attention to a coming conflict (Isa. 20).

—*Be Decisive*, page 89

4. What did God forbid Jeremiah from participating in? (See Jer. 16:1–9.)
Why did God forbid these things for Jeremiah? What message did this give
the followers of God?

From the Commentary

The fourth message was about Judah's sins (Jer. 17:1–27).

President Calvin Coolidge came home from church one
Sunday, and his wife asked, "What did the preacher preach
about?" "Sin," the president said in his usual concise manner. "What did he say about it?" Mrs. Coolidge further
inquired, and the president replied, "He was against it."

Jeremiah was against the sins of his people, six of which
he named in chapter 17.

Idolatry (vv. 1–4).

Unbelief (vv. 5–10).

Greed (v. 11).

Forsaking the Lord (vv. 12–13).

Rejecting God's servant (vv. 14–18).

Profaning the Sabbath (vv. 19–27).

—*Be Decisive*, pages 91–94

5. Review the named sins as listed above. Why do you think each of these sins was singled out? What does this say about the people's sinfulness? About what God was asking them to do? How are these sins still prevalent today?

From Today's World

There are all kinds of prophecies floating around the world today, thanks in part to how easy it is to publicize anything on the Internet. Some prophecies come from outside the Judeo-Christian tradition, such as the prediction of the end of the world based on the Mayan calendar. But most still are anchored in Christianity. Most range from the silly to the dangerous, from predictions about Jesus' return to proclamations of God's judgment and punishment for specific groups of people. There used to be a number of proofs to determine if someone was a true prophet, the most important of which was that he or she was 100 percent accurate. Jeremiah passed that test because God gave him the role, but most of today's so-called prophets fail.

6. What prompts people to become prophets if it's not God's call? Do you think most of them believe what they're preaching? Why or why not? What can we learn from these supposed prophets? What are the dangers of giving too much credence to untested prophets?

From the Commentary

Over thirty words in the Hebrew vocabulary relate directly to pottery, because the manufacture of pottery was a major industry in the Near East in that day. No doubt Jeremiah had passed the potter's house many times, but this time God had a special message for him that, after he preached it, would put him in jail. When you follow the Lord, you never know what will happen to you next.

The potter sat before two parallel stone wheels that were joined by a shaft. He turned the bottom wheel with his feet and worked the clay on the top wheel as the wheel turned. As Jeremiah watched, he saw that the clay resisted the potter's hand so that the vessel was ruined, but the potter patiently kneaded the clay and made another vessel.

The *interpretation* of the image was national, relating to the house of Israel (Jer. 18:6–10), but the *application* was individual (vv. 11–17), calling for a response from the people of Judah and Jerusalem. It also calls for a personal response from us today.

—*Be Decisive*, page 98

7. Read Jeremiah 18:6–10. What does this passage tell us about the interpretation of the pottery image? Read verses 11–17. In what ways is this application of the message directed to the individual? What is the overall message in this prophecy?

From the Commentary

Proud sinners don't enjoy hearing about God's sovereignty or the threat of impending judgment. They think that by silencing the messenger they will silence the Lord. "He who sits in the heavens shall laugh; the Lord shall hold them in derision" (Ps. 2:4 NKJV). Their argument was "We have plenty of priests, prophets, and elders, so we can do without Jeremiah!"

This wasn't the first time Jeremiah had faced a conspiracy that threatened his ministry and his life (Jer. 11:18–23; 12:6; 15:15), and it wouldn't be the last time. His enemies plotted a "smear campaign" consisting of lies about him (see 9:3). The plot probably included quotations from his messages that suggested he was a traitor to the kingdom of Judah. Like the men who plotted against Jesus, Jeremiah's enemies tried to prove he was breaking the law and stirring up the people (Luke 23:1–7).

Faithful servants of God don't enjoy opposition, but they learn to expect it. "In the world you will have tribulation," promised Jesus, "but be of good cheer, I have overcome the world" (John 16:33 NKJV). He also said, "If the world hates you, you know that it hated Me before it hated you" (15:18 NKJV). And Paul reminded Timothy and us, "Yes, and all who desire to live godly in Christ Jesus will suffer persecution" (2 Tim. 3:12 NKJV).

—*Be Decisive*, page 101

8. How is the campaign against Jeremiah similar to what some leaders endure today? How is it different? How did it affect Jeremiah personally? (See Jer. 17:19–23.)

More to Consider: Read the following passages: Ephesians 4:26; Psalm 97:10; Romans 12:9; Mark 3:5; and 2 Corinthians 11:29. What do these verses tell us about righteous anger? How is righteous anger different from regular anger? Why is Jeremiah's anger a righteous anger?

From the Commentary

At the command of the Lord, Jeremiah made a second trip to the potter's house, this time as a customer and not a spectator, and he took with him some of the Jewish elders. Knowing their evil plots against him, it's an evidence of his faith that he was willing to walk with them and then do so daring a thing as declare *in their very presence* that disaster was coming to the land because of their sins. Obviously his prayer to the Lord had brought him peace and courage.

"I will make void the counsel of Judah and Jerusalem in this place" (Jer. 19:7). To demonstrate this, Jeremiah broke a clay jar and said, "This is what the Lord Almighty says: 'I will smash this nation and this city just as this potter's jar is smashed and cannot be repaired'" (v. 11 NIV). The nation was beyond discipline (2:23), beyond prayer (7:16), and now, beyond repair! They had so hardened themselves against the Lord that all hope was gone.

What before had been threats now became a reality. Pashur, son of Immer, assistant to the high priest and chief security officer for the temple, didn't like what Jeremiah was saying. Therefore, he had Jeremiah arrested, beaten, and put into the stocks until the next day. The stocks were located at a prominent place in the temple area, in order to add shame to pain. Spending all night with your body bent and twisted wouldn't be at all comfortable, and when you add the pain of the beating, you can imagine how Jeremiah felt.

—*Be Decisive*, pages 102–4

9. Review Jeremiah 19:1—20:6. What was Jeremiah's state of mind in the midst of this challenging circumstance? What gave him the confidence to speak out? What was he risking to do this? Where was God in the middle of all this?

From the Commentary

Jeremiah 20:7–18 is the last of Jeremiah's recorded laments; it's a human blending of grief and joy, prayer and despair, praise and perplexity. When you call to mind the sensitive nature of this man, you aren't surprised that he's on the mountaintop one minute and in the deepest valley the next. Jeremiah, however, lived above his moods and did the will of God regardless of how he felt. In this honest expression of his deepest emotions, the prophet dealt with three important concerns: God's call (vv. 7–9), his daily peril (vv. 10–13), and his inner despair (vv. 14–18).

—*Be Decisive*, pages 105–6

10. What caused Jeremiah's discouragement? What does it mean to "live above your moods"? How did Jeremiah deal with the three important concerns mentioned in the *Be Decisive* excerpt?

Looking Inward

Take a moment to reflect on all that you've explored thus far in this study of Jeremiah 14—20. Review your notes and answers and think about how each of these things matters in your life today.

Tips for Small Groups: To get the most out of this section, form pairs or trios and have group members take turns answering these questions. Be honest and as open as you can in this discussion, but most of all, be encouraging and supportive of others. Be sensitive to those who are going through particularly difficult times and don't press for people to speak if they're uncomfortable doing so.

11. Jeremiah had the unenviable task of speaking God's truth to a group of people who didn't want to listen. Have you ever had to tell someone a truth he or she didn't want to hear? What was that experience like? When have you been on the other end of that sort of conversation? What made you not want to listen to the truth?

12. If you've ever been tempted to follow a purported prophet, what was it that captured your interest? How do you know when you're following someone who is speaking the truth? What do you use to test the veracity of a speaker's message?

13. Think about a time when you were discouraged like Jeremiah. What led to that discouragement? Did you sense God's presence in the middle of that time? Why or why not? How did you find your way out of that discouragement? How frankly do you talk to God during those times?

Going Forward

14. Think of one or two things that you have learned that you'd like to work on in the coming week. Remember that this is all about quality, not quantity. It's better to work on one specific area of life and do it well than to work on many and do poorly (or to be so overwhelmed that you simply don't try).

Do you need to find a way out of discouragement? Be specific. Go back through Jeremiah 14—20 and put a star next to the phrase or verse that is most encouraging to you. Consider memorizing this verse.

Real-Life Application Ideas: You don't have to look too far to find people who are discouraged in their faith. Perhaps a family member or close friend is going through a difficult time. Spend this week offering a listening ear and appropriate encouragement to those who are discouraged. This isn't a time to "solve" others' discouragement but to join them in the lament and ask God to bring comfort and peace.

Seeking Help

15. Write a prayer below (or simply pray one in silence), inviting God to work on your mind and heart in those areas you've noted in the Going Forward section. Be honest about your desires and fears.

Notes for Small Groups:

- *Look for ways to put into practice the things you wrote in the Going Forward section. Talk with other group members about your ideas and commit to being accountable to one another.*

- *During the coming week, ask the Holy Spirit to continue to reveal truth to you from what you've read and studied.*

- *Before you start the next lesson, read Jeremiah 21—29. For more in-depth lesson preparation, read chapters 7 and 8, "Kings on Parade" and "Facing Truth and Fighting Lies," in* Be Decisive.

Kings and Lies
(JEREMIAH 21—29)

Before you begin ...
- *Pray for the Holy Spirit to reveal truth and wisdom as you go through this lesson.*
- *Read Jeremiah 21—29. This lesson references chapters 7 and 8 in* Be Decisive. *It will be helpful for you to have your Bible and a copy of the commentary available as you work through this lesson.*

Getting Started

From the Commentary

The events in Jeremiah 21:1–14 probably took place in the year 588 BC, when the invincible Babylonian army was camped around the walls of Jerusalem. Hoping to secure help from Egypt, weak King Zedekiah had rebelled against Nebuchadnezzar by refusing to pay tribute (2 Chron. 36:13; see Ezek. 17:11–18); now Judah was suffering the dreadful consequences of his foolish decision. In desperation, he looked to Jeremiah for help by sending Zephaniah the priest and Pashur, one of the court officers, to see whether the prophet could get guidance from the Lord. The king hoped that Jehovah would send a miraculous deliverance to Jerusalem as He had done in the days of godly King Hezekiah (2 Kings 18—19). Jeremiah, however, responded with dire pronouncements to the king (Jer. 21:3–7), to the people (vv. 8–10), and to the house of David (vv. 11–14).

—*Be Decisive*, page 112

1. What must it have been like for Jeremiah to deliver such difficult news to the king? Why did God have dire pronouncements instead of deliverance for the king?

More to Consider: Review the terms of the covenant God had with His people (see Deut. 29:23, 28; 32:16–17, 21; Lev. 26:27–28). In what ways do these terms make God's use of words like anger, fury, *and* great wrath *(Jer. 21:5) to describe His disposition toward His own people seem appropriate? How is God's fury different from a human's?*

2. Choose one verse or phrase from Jeremiah 21—29 that stands out to you. This could be something you're intrigued by, something that makes you uncomfortable, something that puzzles you, something that resonates with you, or just something you want to examine further. Write that here.

Going Deeper

From the Commentary

> Godly King Josiah reigned for thirty-one years and sought to lead the people back to God. But the last four kings of Judah were wicked men, even though three of them were Josiah's sons and one was his grandson (Jehoiachin).
>
> *Jehoahaz*, or Shallum, succeeded Josiah and reigned only three months (Jer. 22:10–12; 2 Kings 23:30–33). Pharaoh Necho deported him to Egypt, where he died.
>
> *Jehoiakim*, also called Eliakim, reigned for eleven years (Jer. 22:13–23; 2 Kings 23:34—24:6) and died in Jerusalem. He was followed by his son *Jehoiachin*, also called Jeconiah and Coniah, whose reign lasted only three months (Jer. 22:24–30; 2 Kings 24:6–12). Nebuchadnezzar took him to Babylon, where eventually he died.

The last king of Judah was *Zedekiah*, who reigned eleven years and saw the kingdom and the Holy City destroyed by Babylon (Jer. 22:1–9; 2 Kings 24:17—25:21). He was blinded and taken to Babylon to die. As Kipling wrote, "The captains and the kings depart."

—*Be Decisive*, page 115

3. Why do you suppose there were so many wicked kings during this period in biblical history? How would this have affected Jeremiah's work? His sense of purpose? His hope?

From the Commentary

Jeremiah denounced all the leaders ("shepherds") of Judah for the ruthless way they treated the helpless people (Jer. 23:1–4). Instead of *leading* the flock in love, they *drove* it mercilessly and exploited it. The shepherds didn't visit ("care for") the sheep, but God would visit the leaders with punishment. Because the leaders disobeyed the law and refused to trust God, they destroyed the nation and scattered the flock among the Gentiles. God, however, promised to regather His people and transform the remnant into a nation. (The word *remnant* is used nineteen times in Jeremiah.) A remnant did return to Judah after the captivity, rebuild the temple, and restore national life.

Jeremiah, however, promised a much greater regathering of the Jews—a greater miracle than their deliverance from Egypt (vv. 7–8; see 16:14–15). God will call His people from the nations of the world, gather them in their land, purge them, and then send them their promised Messiah (Jer. 30; Isa. 2:1–5; 4:1–6; 9:1–7; 11:1—12:6; Zech. 12—14). David's "family tree" might have been cut down, but a "branch" (shoot) would grow from the stump and become Ruler of the nation (Isa. 11:1; 53:2).

—*Be Decisive*, page 119

4. Review Jeremiah 23:1–8. In what ways did the leaders of Judah exploit the people? What caused them to stop trusting God? How would Jeremiah's message of a coming Messiah have been received by the wayward nation?

From the Commentary

> What God said, as recorded in Jeremiah 14:14, summa-
> rizes 23:9–40: "The prophets prophesy lies in My name.
> I have not sent them, commanded them, nor spoken to
> them; they prophesy to you a false vision, divination, a
> worthless thing, and the deceit of their heart" (NKJV).
> Jeremiah focused on three areas in their lives that were
> especially abhorrent.
>
> —*Be Decisive*, page 120

5. Review Jeremiah 23:9–40. What does this passage tell us about the false prophets' conduct? Their message? Their attitude? Why were these so abhorrent to God? What was Jeremiah's answer to the false prophets?

From the Commentary

> In 597 BC, the Babylonians deported King Jehoiachin
> (also called Jeconiah or Coniah) along with many of the
> nobles and key citizens, leaving only the poorer people to
> work the land (2 Kings 24:14–16). It was the beginning

of the end for Judah, and no doubt Jeremiah was greatly distressed.

Knowing that His servant needed encouragement, the Lord gave him a vision of two baskets of figs sitting before the temple of the Lord. One basket held very good figs, the kind that ripened early in the season, and the other basket contained rotten figs, which nobody could eat. Then the Lord explained that the good figs represented the exiles who had just been taken to Babylon, while the bad figs represented King Zedekiah and his officials as well as the survivors who remained in the land or who had fled to Egypt.

What do you do with rotten figs? You reject them and throw them away! What do you do with tasty, good figs? You preserve them and enjoy them! God promised to care for the exiles, work in their hearts, and one day bring them back to their land. Jeremiah even wrote a letter to the exiles, telling them to live peaceably in the land and seek the Lord with all their hearts (Jer. 29:1–14). There was no future for King Zedekiah, who had succeeded Jehoiachin, or for the nobles that gave him such foolish counsel, but there was a future for a godly remnant that would seek the Lord with all their hearts.

—*Be Decisive*, pages 124–25

6. How would the vision of the figs have encouraged Jeremiah during this season? Why did Jeremiah trust God's nearness when so many in Judah did not? What was the difference? How would the prophecy of a

future for a "godly remnant" have been an encouragement for some and discouragement for others?

From the Commentary

> Jeremiah had been serving for twenty-three years when he delivered the messages recorded in chapters 25 and 26 (25:3; 26:1). He was called into prophetic service in the year 626 BC (1:2) and continued to minister after the fall of Jerusalem in 587 BC, a period of over forty years. He was now at the midpoint of his career. When you consider the unsympathetic response of the people both to him and to his messages, you marvel that Jeremiah wasn't discouraged and ready to quit, but he continued to be faithful to his calling.
>
> —*Be Decisive*, pages 129–30

7. What was the message Jeremiah delivered to the Jews (Jer. 25:1–14)? To the Gentile nations (vv. 15–38)? What kept him going, despite apparent failure of his messages to resonate with the people? How is his persistence

and consistency a contrast to many leaders today? What can today's leaders learn from Jeremiah's diligence?

From the Commentary

Chapter 26 of Jeremiah should be studied in connection with chapter 7, because they both deal with Jeremiah's courageous sermon given in the temple. The sermon is summarized in verses 3–7, and you will note the emphasis on *hearing the word of God* (see 25:3–8). Jeremiah preached exactly what God commanded him to preach and didn't alter the message in order to please the people. The false prophets preached what the people *wanted* to hear, but Jeremiah preached what the people *needed* to hear. "Whatsoever I command thee thou shalt speak" (1:7).

The people in the temple, however, encouraged by the priests and false prophets, rejected Jeremiah's message and treated him like a false prophet who deserved to die. To them, it was blasphemous for Jeremiah to declare that Jehovah would allow the Holy City and His holy temple to fall into the defiling and destructive hands of the heathen the way the ark at Shiloh fell into the hands of the Philistines (1 Sam. 4). Since God's covenant with David protected the city and the temple, Jeremiah was actually denying the covenant! He was leading the people astray and deserved to die (Deut. 18:20).

—*Be Decisive*, page 134

8. Do you think Jeremiah was tempted to soften the message given in the temple? Why or why not? What does it say about his relationship with God that he plowed ahead and spoke the words God gave him? What are some parallels to this situation in today's church? Do today's speakers and leaders soften messages to keep from upsetting people? Explain.

From the Commentary

Once again, Jeremiah had to use an "action sermon" to get the attention of the people, and he did it at a time when Zedekiah was conferring with representatives from five neighboring nations. These nations were allies of Judah, and together they were planning a strategy for dealing with Nebuchadnezzar.

A yoke speaks of submission, and that's the message Jeremiah was trying to get across. First, Jeremiah sent the message to *the envoys of the nations* (Jer. 27:1–11). What these politicians needed was not clever strategy but submission to Babylon. When Jeremiah was asked why he was wearing a yoke, he gave them the message from God: Judah and the other nations must submit to Nebuchadnezzar or else be destroyed. God had given the nations to the king of Babylon, and those nations who rebelled against him were rebelling against God (vv. 7–8, 11–12). He sent this message to the envoys gathered in Jerusalem, who certainly had heard about this peculiar Jewish man who was walking around wearing a yoke (see 28:10).

Jeremiah then gave the same message *to King Zedekiah* (Jer. 27:12–15). Since the king had rebelled against Babylon and refused to pay tribute, he was now in serious trouble. When the king saw Jeremiah wearing the yoke, he surely must have gotten the message: "Bring your necks under the yoke of the king of Babylon, and serve him and his people, and live" (v. 12). Jeremiah warned the king not to listen to the deceptive messages of the false prophets, because they were speaking only lies in the name of the Lord.

Jeremiah then delivered the "yoke" message *to the priests and the people* (Jer. 27:16–22). The false prophets were claiming that the valuable articles of gold and bronze that the Babylonians had taken from the temple would soon be returned to Jerusalem, but Jeremiah knew this was a lie. Actually, these treasures weren't brought back until God visited the Jews and the remnant returned to Judah after the decree of Cyrus (Ezra 1—2). The important thing wasn't to rescue the temple furnishings but to save the people from death and the city from destruction. This could be done only if the nation submitted to the king of Babylon.

Jeremiah ended his message to the priests and people with a promise of hope: At the end of their captivity, God would visit His people in Babylon and bring them back to their land. Even in wrath, God remembers mercy (Hab. 3:2).

While Jeremiah was wearing the yoke and calling the nation to submit to Babylon, Hananiah, one of the false prophets, confronted him in the temple. About this same time, according to historians, Nebuchadnezzar was putting down a revolt in his own land. Hananiah wrongly interpreted the uprising as the end of Nebuchadnezzar's rule. Hananiah announced that God had broken the yoke of the king of Babylon and that the temple treasures would be returned to Jerusalem within two years. More than that, King Jeconiah and all the exiles would be returned with them.

These messages contradicted what Jeremiah had spoken in the name of the Lord. The Lord had told Jeremiah that the deported people and the temple vessels wouldn't be restored to the land until He visited the exiles at the end of their captivity (Jer. 27:16—22). Furthermore, King

Jeconiah would never return to Judah but would die in Babylon (22:24–27; 52:31–34).

—*Be Decisive*, pages 135–38

9. Review Jeremiah 27:1—28:17. There's a lot going on in these verses. How did Jeremiah's "action sermon" (the wearing of a yoke) get the people's attention? Did it accomplish the task of spurring them to appropriate action? What are some ways leaders today use similar "props" to make a point? What challenges did Jeremiah face in this section that he hadn't faced before?

From the Commentary

Several different letters are included in Jeremiah 29: a letter from Jeremiah to the exiles (vv. 1–14); a letter concerning Jewish false prophets in Babylon to which Jeremiah replied (vv. 15–23); a letter from Shemaiah to the temple priests concerning Jeremiah, which he read (vv. 24–29); and a letter from Jeremiah to the exiles concerning Shemaiah (vv. 30–32). Correspondence like this wasn't difficult to maintain in those days, for there were regular diplomatic missions between Jerusalem and Babylon (v. 3), and Jeremiah had friends in high places in the government.

—*Be Decisive*, page 139

10. What was Jeremiah's word of encouragement in chapter 29 (see vv. 1–14)? What was his explanation (see vv. 15–23)? What was the warning he gave (see vv. 24–32)? How encouraging would it have been to have a future that would be fulfilled decades later? Why?

Looking Inward

Take a moment to reflect on all that you've explored thus far in this study of Jeremiah 21—29. Review your notes and answers and think about how each of these things matters in your life today.

Tips for Small Groups: To get the most out of this section, form pairs or trios and have group members take turns answering these questions. Be honest and as open as you can in this discussion, but most of all, be encouraging and supportive of others. Be sensitive to those who are going through particularly difficult times and don't press for people to speak if they're uncomfortable doing so.

11. Have you ever felt exploited or used by a person in a leadership position? What led to that circumstance? How did you respond to the leader's attempt to use you? What are the differences between being exploited by a leader and being properly shepherded?

12. Jeremiah was known to be dramatic when presenting his messages. What's the greatest length you've gone to get a point across? How did that work for you? Did it inspire people to listen? Did it backfire? What did you learn from the situation?

13. Have you ever been tempted to soften the truth when confronting someone? If so, did you give in to that temptation? Why or why not? Why is it difficult to speak the truth when people don't want to hear it?

Going Forward

14. Think of one or two things that you have learned that you'd like to work on in the coming week. Remember that this is all about quality, not quantity. It's better to work on one specific area of life and do it well than to work on many and do poorly (or to be so overwhelmed that you simply don't try).

Do you want to strengthen your resolve for speaking the truth to others? Be specific. Go back through Jeremiah 21—29 and put a star next to the phrase or verse that is most encouraging to you. Consider memorizing this verse.

Real-Life Application Ideas: Spend this week building your knowledge and understanding of common disagreements people have with Christianity. Talk casually with friends who aren't believers to learn what turns them off about Christianity. Listen to arguments and complaints without seeking to immediately confront them. Then spend time in study, looking for godly responses to each of the concerns. If God leads you to return to some of those folks to talk about where you stand, then by all means follow that path. But if not, use this experience to shore up your faith in anticipation of those coming interactions you don't yet know God is preparing you for.

Seeking Help

15. Write a prayer below (or simply pray one in silence), inviting God to work on your mind and heart in those areas you've noted in the Going Forward section. Be honest about your desires and fears.

Notes for Small Groups:

- *Look for ways to put into practice the things you wrote in the Going Forward section. Talk with other group members about your ideas and commit to being accountable to one another.*

- *During the coming week, ask the Holy Spirit to continue to reveal truth to you from what you've read and studied.*

- *Before you start the next lesson, read Jeremiah 30—33. For more in-depth lesson preparation, read chapter 9, "The God Who Makes Things New," in* Be Decisive.

All Things New
(JEREMIAH 30—33)

Before you begin ...
- *Pray for the Holy Spirit to reveal truth and wisdom as you go through this lesson.*
- *Read Jeremiah 30—33. This lesson references chapter 9 in* Be Decisive. *It will be helpful for you to have your Bible and a copy of the commentary available as you work through this lesson.*

Getting Started

From the Commentary

Bible scholars often call these four chapters the "Book of Consolation." In them, the Lord amplified the wonderful promise He gave to His people in the letter Jeremiah sent the Babylonian exiles: "'For I know the plans I have for you,' declares the Lord, 'plans to prosper you and not to harm you, plans to give you hope and a future'" (Jer. 29:11 NIV).

Jeremiah 30—33 describes the glory of the dawning of a new day for the people of Israel, not only for the exiles in Babylon but also for the Jewish people in the latter days before the Lord returns. As you study, you'll discover that Jeremiah had two horizons in view: the nearer horizon of the return of the exiles to Judah and the farther horizon of the regathering of Israel in the end times from the nations of the earth.

—*Be Decisive*, pages 145–46

1. Read Jeremiah 29:11 again. In what ways would this message have been a great comfort to the Jews? How does this same message resonate with believers even today?

2. Choose one verse or phrase from Jeremiah 30—33 that stands out to you. This could be something you're intrigued by, something that makes you uncomfortable, something that puzzles you, something that resonates with you, or just something you want to examine further. Write that here.

Going Deeper

From the Commentary

Jeremiah received the words recorded in 30:1—31:25 while he was asleep (31:26), for God sometimes spoke to His servants through dreams (Dan. 10:9; Zech. 4:1). God instructed Jeremiah to write His words in a book (scroll) so the nation would have a permanent record of the promises God was giving to His people (see Jer. 36:1–4).

In His instructions to Jeremiah, God stated the theme of His message: Israel (the northern kingdom, taken by Assyria in 722 BC) and Judah (the southern kingdom) will eventually return to their land as a united people (30:3). While this promise refers ultimately to the regathering of the Jews at the end of the age, it certainly was an encouragement to the exiles in Babylon, for if God can gather His people from *all* the nations of the world, surely He can deliver Judah from the captivity of *one* nation.

—*Be Decisive*, page 146

3. What was Jeremiah's promise in chapter 30 (see v. 10)? Why was the message of a "regathering" so important to the formerly divided kingdom? How did this provide hope to the exiles?

From the Commentary

The redemption of God's people from bondage is pictured in several ways.

To summarize: The people of Judah and Jerusalem will experience terrible trials at the hands of the Babylonians. They will end up wearing the Gentile yoke, bearing the wounds caused by their sins, and having endured the storm of God's wrath. But God would eventually deliver them, breaking the yoke, healing the wounds, and bringing peace after the storm. All of this will be a foreshadowing of what will happen to the Jews in the end times as they go through the tribulation, meet their Messiah-King, and enter into their kingdom.

—*Be Decisive*, pages 146, 148

4. How did Jeremiah use each of the following images to speak truth to God's people: the yoke (Jer. 30:4–11), the healed wound (vv. 12–17), the calm after the storm (vv. 18–24)? In what ways was Jeremiah speaking about their current circumstances? Their future hope? Why were both messages important?

From Today's World

God's chosen people were entering a time of great tribulation as the exile to Babylon began. Jeremiah had prophesied about their captivity, but also about a future that was full of hope and promise. Today's church is in a much different place in history, but trials and challenges still confront believers both in America and abroad. In some countries, persecution continues to threaten Christians. In others, the divide between religions is growing, building an environment that is often contentious and sometimes even deadly.

5. How is the church today in "exile"? Who are the captors? What are the risks and challenges of living out Christian beliefs around the world today? How might Jeremiah's message to the broken nation about a future hope apply also to today's church?

From the Commentary

A nation is more than its land and cities; it's people living together, working together, and worshipping together. In chapter 31, Jeremiah described the people of God and the new things the Lord would do for them. He first spoke to a united nation (vv. 1, 27–30), then to Israel (vv. 2–20), and finally to Judah (vv. 21–26).

Because of the sins of Solomon and the foolishness of his son Rehoboam, the Jewish nation divided and became Israel and Judah, the northern kingdom and the southern kingdom (1 Kings 11—12). But in the last days, the Lord will gather His people, unite them, and be the "God of all the families of Israel" (Jer. 31:1). In fact, God compared Israel and Judah to seed that will be sown in the land and produce one harvest, not two (v. 27).

The names "Ephraim" and "Samaria" are references to the northern kingdom of Israel, whose capital was at Samaria (Jer. 31:4–6, 9, 18, 20). The people of the northern kingdom were captured in 722 BC by the Assyrians, who brought other peoples into the land so as to produce a mixed race (2 Kings 17). When the people of Judah returned to their land from the captivity, they would have nothing to do with the Samaritans (Ezra 4:1–4; Neh. 2:19–20; 13:28), a practice that persisted into New Testament times (John 4:9). Subsequently, the Samaritans established their own religion, temple, and priesthood, and this alienated the Jews even more.

As the Jews started for Babylon, God instructed them to remember the roads and set up markers along the route, for the people would use those same roads when they return to their land. Jeremiah pictured Judah as a silly girl, flitting from lover to lover, and now summoned to come home. (He used this image before. See 2:1–2, 20;

3:1–11.) According to the law, a daughter who prostituted herself should have been killed (Lev. 21:9; Deut. 22:21), but God would do a new thing: He would welcome her home and forgive her!

—Be Decisive, pages 148–50

6. How was God's promise of a united kingdom and a new future intended to help the soon-to-be-exiled Jews "take their punishment" gracefully? What might they have been thinking as they heard this message? Did they believe they deserved a worse fate? Why or why not?

From the Commentary

Any plan for the betterment of human society that ignores the sin problem is destined to failure. It isn't enough to change the environment, for the heart of every problem is the problem of the heart. God must change the hearts of people so that they want to love Him and do His will. That's why He announced a new covenant to replace the old covenant under which the Jews had lived since the days of Moses, a covenant that could direct their conduct but not change their character.

Jewish history is punctuated with a number of covenant renewals that brought temporary blessing but didn't change the hearts of the people. The book of Deuteronomy records a renewal of the covenant under Moses, before the people entered the Promised Land. In addition, before he died, Joshua led the people in reaffirming the covenant (Josh. 23—24). Samuel called the nation to renew their vows to God (1 Sam. 12), and both Hezekiah (2 Chron. 29—31) and Josiah (2 Chron. 34—35) inspired great days of "revival" as they led the people back to God's law.

The fact that the blessings didn't last is no argument against times of revival and refreshing.

—*Be Decisive*, page 151

7. What is the new covenant described in Jeremiah 31:31–40? How can a new covenant inspire revival? Why did the covenant need to be renewed from time to time? What does this say about God's people? About God Himself?

From the Commentary

> The basis for the new covenant is the work of Jesus Christ on the cross (Matt. 26:27–28; Mark 14:22–24; Luke 22:19–20).
>
> The Lord affirmed the permanence of the nation and the faithfulness of His relationship to His people (Jer. 31:35–37). It would be easier for the sun to stop shining and the moon and stars to go out than for God to break His promises to His people Israel. Just as Jerusalem was rebuilt after the Babylonian captivity, so it will be restored after the time of Jacob's trouble and be holy to the Lord. Because of its ancient associations with Israel, Islam, Jesus, and the church, Jerusalem is called "the Holy City," but it will not truly be holy until the Lord restores it and reigns in glory at the end of the age.
>
> —*Be Decisive*, page 152

8. In what ways does today's church partake in Israel's spiritual riches? (See Rom. 11:12–32; Eph. 3:1–6.) How do Christians today share in the new covenant described in Jeremiah? (See Heb. 8:6–13; 10:14–18.)

From the Commentary

> It wasn't enough for the prophet merely to preach God's promises; he also had to practice them and prove to his hearers that he believed them himself. "Faith without works is dead" (James 2:26). Therefore, God directed Jeremiah to give another "action sermon" and purchase a piece of property at a time when the fortunes of Judah couldn't have been lower. In so doing, Jeremiah got the attention of the people and was able to affirm God's great promises to them.
>
> —*Be Decisive*, pages 152–53

9. How did Jeremiah "put his money where his mouth is" by purchasing land? What does this say about the role of trust in our relationship with God? How is this an example of what is taught in James 2:26?

More to Consider: The basic theme of Jeremiah's prayer in 32:26–44 is "Nothing is too hard for you" (v. 17), and God reaffirmed that very truth to His servant (v. 27). Where did Jeremiah get such confidence? What role does good theology play in confidence? (See Rom. 10:17.)

From the Commentary

"Call to me and I will answer you and tell you great and unsearchable things you do not know" (Jer. 33:3 NIV). The word translated "unsearchable" pictures an impregnable city protected by high walls—an apt image during the siege of Jerusalem. The idea is that God's people don't learn the hidden things of the Lord by "storming the gates" through their own strength but by seeking Him through believing prayer. Because Jeremiah asked the Lord to teach him, God showed him "hidden things" that related to the future of his people. The prophet knew that the city was destined for judgment (vv. 4–5), but the Lord gave him further words of assurance and encouragement—promises that relate to the end times.

The defiled nation would be healed and cleansed (vv. 6–8) and the disgraceful city would bring joy and renown to the Lord and be a testimony to all the nations of the world of the marvelous goodness and grace of God (v. 9). The deserted city would one day be filled with people praising the Lord and expressing their joy to one another (vv. 10–11). The pasture lands, ruined by devastating judgment, would one day be full of flocks and herds, and the little towns would once more enjoy happiness (vv. 12–13). Since these blessings didn't come during the post-exilic period, we have to believe they'll be realized when the Lord returns and restores His people and their land.

The greatest blessing of all will be their promised King reigning in righteousness (vv. 14–16; see 23:5)! Jeremiah already told us that His name is "The Lord our Righteousness" (v. 6), but now God revealed that *Jerusalem will bear the same name*! That certainly didn't happen when the exiles returned to rebuild their temple and their city. Therefore, this promise is for the latter days. Then when people call Jerusalem "the Holy City," the name will be appropriate.

Once again, the Lord used the faithfulness of His creation covenant (Gen. 8:22) to undergird the dependability of His promises and the perpetuity of His people (Jer. 33:19–26; see 31:35–37). But He adds something else: He will multiply the people as the stars of the heaven, which was one of the promises He had made to Abraham (Gen. 15:1–5).

—*Be Decisive*, pages 155–56

10. Why was the promise of a righteous king so appealing to the exiles? Would they have expected this king to appear in their lifetime? How would this affect their trust in God? What does this entire section (Jer. 33) reveal to us about God's pursuit of His people? The people's hope?

Looking Inward

Take a moment to reflect on all that you've explored thus far in this study of Jeremiah 30—33. Review your notes and answers and think about how each of these things matters in your life today.

Tips for Small Groups: To get the most out of this section, form pairs or trios and have group members take turns answering these questions. Be honest and as open as you can in this discussion, but most of all, be encouraging and supportive of others. Be sensitive to those who are going through particularly difficult times and don't press for people to speak if they're uncomfortable doing so.

11. God's people suffered lots of trials and tribulations in Jeremiah's day. While this was often the result of their sins, it certainly had to take its toll on them. What are some of the hardest things you've had to deal with in your faith journey? How have these things discouraged you? What message has God spoken to you during these times?

12. In some ways, Jeremiah's message to the departing Jews was simply "Hang in there—it gets better." What are some ways you're "hanging in

there" in your own faith story? What hopes do you cling to for your life here on earth and beyond?

13. How are you encouraging others who are currently suffering? What are some ways you can be a Jeremiah to them, providing hope for a brighter future?

Going Forward

14. Think of one or two things that you have learned that you'd like to work on in the coming week. Remember that this is all about quality, not quantity. It's better to work on one specific area of life and do it well than to work on many and do poorly (or to be so overwhelmed that you simply don't try).

Do you need to discover hope in the midst of challenging times? Be specific. Go back through Jeremiah 30—33 and put a star next to the phrase or verse that is most encouraging to you. Consider memorizing this verse.

Real-Life Application Ideas: Think about the circumstances in your life that tend to discourage you. Perhaps it's a job situation or challenges at home. God is perfectly aware of all that you're struggling with. Write a letter of encouragement to yourself, similar to something Jeremiah might have written if he were prophesying about your life. This is harder than it sounds. Be brutally honest (as Jeremiah was) but also full of encouragement. Then read this letter daily for a week to remind yourself that God is intimately involved in your life, whatever the circumstances.

Seeking Help

15. Write a prayer below (or simply pray one in silence), inviting God to work on your mind and heart in those areas you've noted in the Going Forward section. Be honest about your desires and fears.

Notes for Small Groups:

- *Look for ways to put into practice the things you wrote in the Going Forward section. Talk with other group members about your ideas and commit to being accountable to one another.*

- *During the coming week, ask the Holy Spirit to continue to reveal truth to you from what you've read and studied.*

- *Before you start the next lesson, read Jeremiah 34—45; 52. For more in-depth lesson preparation, read chapters 10 and 11, "Contemporary Events and Eternal Truths" and "Tragedy Follows Tragedy," in* Be Decisive.

Truth and Tragedy
(JEREMIAH 34—45; 52)

Before you begin …

- *Pray for the Holy Spirit to reveal truth and wisdom as you go through this lesson.*
- *Read Jeremiah 34—45; 52. This lesson references chapters 10 and 11 in* Be Decisive. *It will be helpful for you to have your Bible and a copy of the commentary available as you work through this lesson.*

Getting Started

From the Commentary

In spite of the longsuffering of God and the faithful ministry of God's prophets, the kingdom of Judah was about to die. It was a nation with a glorious heritage—laws given from heaven by Moses, a land conquered by Joshua, a kingdom established by David and made magnificent by Solomon, a people in whose midst Jehovah dwelt in a splendid temple—and yet that glorious heritage couldn't prevent Judah's shameful ruin at the hands of the idolatrous Babylonians. The end had come.

What caused Judah's slow decay and final collapse? The historian would point to their unwise politics, particularly depending on Egypt for help, and we can't deny that Judah's leaders made some stupid decisions. But behind their unwise politics was a more insidious reason: *The leaders really didn't believe the word of God.* During the dramatic rise and fall of empires in that stormy era, Judah looked *around* for allies instead of looking *up* for divine assistance. Instead of repenting and turning to God, they hardened their hearts against the Word and trusted their own wisdom.

—*Be Decisive*, pages 159–60

1. What were some of the events from Judah's final days that Jeremiah noted in these chapters? What were the people of Judah supposed to learn from these events? What do these events teach us about how we treat God? About how our treatment of God affects the world in which we live?

2. Choose one verse or phrase from Jeremiah 34—45; 52 that stands out to you. This could be something you're intrigued by, something that makes you uncomfortable, something that puzzles you, something that resonates with you, or just something you want to examine further. Write that here.

Going Deeper

From the Commentary

> According to the law of Moses, a Jewish master had to free his Jewish slaves at the end of seven years of service (Ex. 21:1–11; Deut. 15:12–18). The Jews hadn't done this for years, and now they decided it was a good thing to do. Why? Perhaps they felt that God would honor their obedience and defeat the enemy in some miraculous way, as He had done for Hezekiah (Isa. 36—37). Instead of believing God's Word and submitting to Babylon, the Jews tried to bargain with the Lord and "bribe" Him into helping their cause.

> Of course, there were probably some practical considerations behind this covenant. If the slaves were free, they'd have to care for themselves; their masters wouldn't have to feed them or care for them. Also freemen were more likely

to want to fight the enemy and maintain their newfound freedom. Whatever the reason, the effects of the covenant didn't last very long, for when there was a lull in the siege and Nebuchadnezzar went off to confront the Egyptian army (Jer. 34:21–22; 37:5–11), the masters all forced their slaves back into servitude. The solemn covenant made in the temple meant nothing.

Before we condemn these dishonest masters too much, let's admit that God's people often make promises to the Lord when they're in tough times, only to repudiate them when things get better.

—*Be Decisive*, page 161

3. What are some of the promises Christians make today because of tough times? Do most people do this out of sincerity, or out of fear? How does God respond to unfulfilled promises?

From the Commentary

The fourth year of Jehoiakim was 605 BC, the year of the fateful Battle of Carchemish when Pharaoh Necho defeated King Josiah and made Judah a vassal to Egypt (Jer. 46:2; 2 Chron. 35:20–27). Jehoiakim had gotten his throne only because Egypt had deposed his brother Jehoahaz. Jeremiah had been ministering for twenty-three years, and now God commanded him to write his messages in a scroll so they would be permanent and could be read by others. Note that his messages dealt with Israel, Judah, and all the nations, and when he wrote the second scroll, he added other material (Jer. 36:32). The first forty-five chapters of the book of Jeremiah focus primarily on Israel and Judah, while chapters 46 to 51 deal with the other nations in the Near East.

—*Be Decisive*, page 163

4. Why did God decide Jeremiah had to write down His messages in a scroll? Why wasn't this the case earlier? What was the message Jeremiah wrote down? (See Jer. 36.)

More to Consider: King Zedekiah was revealed as an incredibly indecisive king. How was his vacillation similar to another leader, Pontius Pilate (see John 18—19)? How can indecisiveness in leadership positions affect a nation?

From the Commentary

Jeremiah 39 and 52, along with 2 Kings 25 and 2 Chronicles 36, describe the tragic fall of Jerusalem, its plunder, and its destruction, as well as the captivity and deportation of thousands of Jewish people. None of these things would have happened if only one of the kings had sincerely repented, trusted the Lord, and surrendered to the Babylonians.

The siege had begun on January 15, 588 BC (Jer. 52:4); and two and a half years later, on July 18, 586 BC, the Babylonian army penetrated the city walls. The princes of Babylon set up their thrones in the Middle Gate and began to take over the reins of government. The "times of the Gentiles" had begun on God's prophetic calendar (Luke 21:24). When that period ends, the Messiah will return to rescue His people and fulfill the promises made by the prophets.

The Lord moved upon Nebuchadnezzar to release the prophet and treat him kindly. He was committed to Gedaliah, who later was named governor of the land (Jer. 40:7). (This Gedaliah was not the one who wanted to kill Jeremiah, 38:1.)

—*Be Decisive*, pages 169–70

5. Review Jeremiah 6:6; 19:8–15; 21:10; 26:6, 11; 27:17. What was the consistent message Jeremiah was giving to the people? How did God keep His promise that Jeremiah would survive the persecution against him? (See also Jer. 1:17–19; 15:20–21; 39:8–10; 52:12–34.)

From the Commentary

Jeremiah was given his freedom after the Babylonians captured Jerusalem (Jer. 39:11–14), but somehow he got mixed in with the captives who were being readied at Ramah for their long march to Babylon. He was released and given the choice of going to Babylon and being cared for by the king or remaining in the land to care for the people.

The Babylonian captain of the guard preached a sermon that sounded a great deal like what Jeremiah had been saying for forty years! It must have been embarrassing for the Jews to hear a pagan Babylonian tell them they were sinners, but he was right in what he said. As God's people, we have to bow in shame when the world publicly announces the sins of the saints (Gen. 12:10–20; 20:1ff.; 2 Sam. 12:14).

Jeremiah chose to join Gedaliah, whom Nebuchadnezzar had appointed governor of the land. Had the people followed the prophet and the governor, the Jewish remnant could have led safe and fairly comfortable lives even in the midst of ruin, but they chose not to obey. Even a severe chastening like the one Babylon brought to Judah didn't change their hearts, for the human heart can be changed only by the grace of God.

—*Be Decisive*, page 174

6. Why did Jeremiah choose to stay with the people? (See Jer. 40:5–6.) Why is it significant that a Babylonian called the people sinners, when Jeremiah had been preaching the same message all along? Why were the people's hearts so hardened to God during this season in history?

From the Commentary

When the good news got out that Gedaliah was in charge of affairs in Judah, the people who had fled and hidden because of the siege began to come back to the land (Jer. 40:7, 11–12). Gedaliah was a good man from a good family, although events proved that he was very naive about practical politics.

Gedaliah told the people exactly what Jeremiah had been telling them for many years: Serve the Babylonians, and you will live safely in the land. The people couldn't reap any harvest of grain because the fields hadn't been sown during the siege, but they could gather the produce that had not been destroyed in the war. The remnant in Judah had to follow the same instructions that Jeremiah gave to the exiles in Babylon: Live normal lives, turn to the Lord with all your hearts, and wait for the Lord to deliver you (29:4–14). God had promised a future for the nation because the nation had important work to do.

—*Be Decisive*, page 175

7. Why was Gedaliah's message so similar to Jeremiah's? How did God use the governor appointed by the Babylonians to move His plans forward? What are other examples of God using political leaders to accomplish a holy purpose?

From the Commentary

Johanan was once brave enough to want to kill Ishmael, but now he didn't have the courage to stand for what he knew was right. He was afraid to trust the Lord and stay in the land of Judah, perhaps because he feared what the Babylonians might do when they found out that Gedaliah was dead and Ishmael had filled a pit with dead bodies.

Their request to Jeremiah sounded sincere and spiritual, but there was deception in the hearts of the leaders, including Johanan (see Jer. 42:19–22). They had their minds already made up to go to Egypt, and they were hoping Jeremiah would agree with them. Sometimes God's people take this false approach in discerning the will of God. Instead of honestly seeking God's will, they go from counselor to counselor, asking for advice and hoping they'll find somebody who will agree with their hidden agenda.

The Lord kept the people waiting for ten days, possibly to give them time to search their hearts and confess their sins. During those ten days, they could see that the Lord was caring for them and that they had nothing to fear. That should have convinced them that the plan to flee to Egypt was a foolish one.

—*Be Decisive*, page 177

8. Why did the people want to leave Judah? Why did they speak to Jeremiah if their minds were already made up? How is the way these leaders acted similar to the way leaders sometimes act in today's church?

From the Commentary

Chapter 44 is Jeremiah's last recorded message to his people, given in Egypt probably in the year 580 BC. If he was called by God in 626, the thirteenth year of Josiah's reign (1:2), then he had been ministering forty-six years. You can't help admiring Jeremiah for his faithfulness in spite of all the discouragements that had come to his life.

No sooner did the Jewish remnant arrive in Egypt than they began to worship the local gods and goddesses, of which there were many. Jeremiah reminded them of *what they had seen* in the Lord's judgment on Judah (44:2–3). It was because of their idolatry that He had destroyed their land, the city of Jerusalem, and the temple. Then he reminded them of *what they had heard*—the messages of the prophets God had sent to rebuke them time after time (vv. 4–6).

But they hadn't learned their lesson, and now they were jeopardizing their future and inviting the wrath of God by repeating in Egypt the sins they'd committed in Judah. Had they forgotten the past? Were they unconcerned about their future? Didn't they realize that God could judge them in Egypt as easily as He had judged them in their own land? No wonder God called the Jews in the land "bad figs that nobody could eat." The future would rest with the exiles in Babylon who would one day return to their land and carry on the work God had given them to do.

—*Be Decisive*, page 180

9. Why did the remnant think they could escape God's judgment in Egypt? Why did they so quickly return to worshipping idols? What prompts people to make poor decisions like these, in spite of all the evidence and history suggesting God's way is the better way?

From the Commentary

Jeremiah 45 gives us insight into the man Baruch. As we noted earlier, he had a brother on the king's official staff who probably could have secured a good job for him in the palace. Instead, Baruch chose to identify with Jeremiah and do the will of God. We thank God for all that Jeremiah did, but we should also thank God for the assistance Baruch gave Jeremiah so the prophet could do his work. Moses had his seventy elders; David had his mighty men; Jesus had His disciples; Paul had his helpers, such as Timothy, Titus, and Silas; and Jeremiah had his faithful secretary.

Not everybody is called to be a prophet or apostle, but all of us can do the will of God by helping others do their work. Baruch was what we'd today call a "layman." Yet he helped a prophet write the Word of God. In my own ministry, I've appreciated the labors of faithful secretaries and assistants who have helped me in myriads of ways. I may have been on the platform, but without their assistance behind the scenes, I could never have gotten my work done. Baruch was willing to stay in the background and serve God by serving Jeremiah.

Another lesson emerges: Even the most devoted servants occasionally get discouraged. Baruch came to a point in his life where he was so depressed that he wanted to quit. "Woe is me now! For the Lord has added grief to my sorrow. I fainted in my sighing, and I find no rest" (45:3 NKJV). Perhaps the persecution of Jeremiah recorded in chapter 26 was the cause of this anguish. Maybe Baruch was considering leaving Jeremiah and asking his brother for an easier job in the palace.

The Lord, however, had a word of encouragement for His servant. First, He cautioned him not to build his hopes on the future of Judah, because everything would be destroyed in the Babylonian siege. A "soft job" in the government would lead only to death or exile in Babylon. Then God gave him a word of assurance: his life would be spared, so he didn't have to fear the enemy. God was proving to Baruch the reality of a promise that would be written centuries later: "But seek first the kingdom of God and His righteousness, and all these things shall be added to you" (Matt. 6:33 NKJV).

—*Be Decisive*, pages 182–83

10. How is Baruch's service to Jeremiah an inspiration for church members today? What does his example teach us about humility? About serving others? What was Baruch's driving reason to stick with Jeremiah all those years? How was God glorified through his work?

Looking Inward

Take a moment to reflect on all that you've explored thus far in this study of Jeremiah 34—45; 52. Review your notes and answers and think about how each of these things matters in your life today.

Tips for Small Groups: To get the most out of this section, form pairs or trios and have group members take turns answering these questions. Be honest and as open as you can in this discussion, but most of all, be encouraging and supportive of others. Be sensitive to those who are going through particularly difficult times and don't press for people to speak if they're uncomfortable doing so.

11. What are some of the promises you've made to God in the heat of the moment that you later broke? Why did you make those promises in the first place? What did you learn through those experiences? Why is it important to follow through with your promises after times are no longer difficult? How can you stay motivated to do this?

12. These chapters of Jeremiah reveal a way God can speak through nonbelievers. What are some of the ways God has spoken to you through

non-Christians? Why does God choose to do that? What does this say about God? About Christians?

13. The remnant that escaped to Egypt made a poor decision even with all the evidence telling them otherwise. What are some of the poor decisions you have made, even when you knew God wanted you to make a different decision? What tempts you away from trusting God? How do you find your way back after you've "escaped to Egypt"?

Going Forward

14. Think of one or two things that you have learned that you'd like to work on in the coming week. Remember that this is all about quality, not quantity. It's better to work on one specific area of life and do it well than to work on many and do poorly (or to be so overwhelmed that you simply don't try).

Do you want to learn how to trust God's guidance even when you feel tempted to run away? Be specific. Go back through Jeremiah 34—45; 52 and put a star next to the phrase or verse that is most encouraging to you. Consider memorizing this verse.

Real-Life Application Ideas: One thing we learn through Jeremiah's story is his consistent dedication to the task God has given him. For many decades, he served God in a job that was far from glamorous and often extremely difficult. Think about your own commitments (to family, work, church, etc.). What are some ways you're like Jeremiah? Celebrate those. What are some ways you tend to be more fickle? How can God use you in both of these circumstances? Consider places in your life where you might develop more roots, more consistency of purpose. Work on those, but keep one eye out for God's ability to surprise. God may have called you to a lifelong dedication to one area of ministry, or He may call you to many.

Seeking Help

15. Write a prayer below (or simply pray one in silence), inviting God to work on your mind and heart in those areas you've noted in the Going Forward section. Be honest about your desires and fears.

Notes for Small Groups:

- *Look for ways to put into practice the things you wrote in the Going Forward section. Talk with other group members about your ideas and commit to being accountable to one another.*

- *During the coming week, ask the Holy Spirit to continue to reveal truth to you from what you've read and studied.*

- *Before you start the next lesson, read Jeremiah 46—51. For more in-depth lesson preparation, read chapters 12 and 13, "God Speaks to the Nations" and "Babylon Is Fallen!" in* Be Decisive.

God Speaks
(JEREMIAH 46—51)

Before you begin …
- *Pray for the Holy Spirit to reveal truth and wisdom as you go through this lesson.*
- *Read Jeremiah 46—51. This lesson references chapters 12 and 13 in* Be Decisive. *It will be helpful for you to have your Bible and a copy of the commentary available as you work through this lesson.*

Getting Started

From the Commentary

Jeremiah had spoken to his people for over forty years, but they wouldn't listen; now he spoke to the nations related in some way to the Jewish people. As God's spokesman, Jeremiah was "handing the cup" to these nations (Jer. 25:15ff.) and declaring what God had planned for them. He was called to be "a prophet unto the nations" (1:5), and he was fulfilling his ministry.

While these names, places, and events are ancient history to most of us, the lessons behind these events reveal to us the hand of God in the rise and fall of rulers and nations. One of the repeated phrases in these chapters is God's "I will," for "history is His story," as A. T. Pierson used to say. You will also note that God judged *the gods of these nations*, just as He had judged the gods of Egypt before Israel's exodus (Ex. 12:12).

—*Be Decisive*, pages 187–88

1. Go through these chapters and circle or underline God's "I will" statements. What do these tell us about God's role in the history of all nations? How does this play out in our world today?

2. Choose one verse or phrase from Jeremiah 46—51 that stands out to you. This could be something you're intrigued by, something that makes you uncomfortable, something that puzzles you, something that resonates with you, or just something you want to examine further. Write that here.

Going Deeper

From the Commentary

> Pharaoh Necho had defeated Judah and killed King Josiah at Megiddo in 609 BC (2 Chron. 35:20–27), but then Nebuchadnezzar defeated Necho at the famous Battle of Carchemish in 605 BC, the fourth year of Jehoiakim. That defeat broke the power of Egypt and made Babylon supreme in the Near East. Jeremiah described the battle from Egypt's viewpoint (Jer. 46:3–12); then he described Babylon's invasion of Egypt (vv. 13–26), concluding with an application to the people of Israel (vv. 27–28).
>
> —*Be Decisive*, page 188

3. Review Jeremiah 46. Summarize the defeat of Egypt. Why was Babylon triumphant? How was this important in God's unfolding story of His people? What assurance did these events give Israel? (See vv. 27–28.)

From the Commentary

The Philistine people probably came from Crete (Caphtor, v. 4). They built a wealthy nation by developing a merchant marine that sailed the Mediterranean and acquired goods from many lands. But their destiny was destruction. Tyre and Sidon had been confederate with Judah in an attempt to stop Nebuchadnezzar (Jer. 27:3).

This time Jeremiah used the image of the rising river to describe the Babylonian army as it flooded over the land (47:2). So terrible was the invasion that parents would flee for their lives and leave their children behind (v. 3; see 49:11). The people would act like mourners at a funeral (47:5) and ask the Lord when He would put up the terrible sword of His judgment (v. 6). But this sword would continue to devour the land until God's work of judgment was finished.

The Moabites were descendants of Lot (Gen. 19:20–38) and, along with the Ammonites, the enemies of the Jews. During the Babylonian crisis, however, both Moab and Ammon allied themselves with Judah in an ill-fated attempt to defeat Nebuchadnezzar (Jer. 27:3). Over twenty different places are named in Jeremiah 48, some of which we can't identify with certainty, but the list shows how detailed God can be when He wants to predict future events.

Like the Moabites, the Ammonites were the product of Lot's incestuous union with one of his daughters (Gen. 19:20–38) and the enemies of the Jews.

—*Be Decisive*, pages 190, 192

4. Describe the different judgments on these nations: Philistia (Jer. 47), Moab (Jer. 48), Ammon (Jer. 49). What do these judgments tell us about each of these nations? About nations in general? About God?

More to Consider: The judgment on Edom (Jer. 49:7–22) is also recorded in the book of Obadiah. Since we don't know when the book of Obadiah was written, we aren't sure whether Jeremiah borrowed from Obadiah or vice versa. Take a few moments to compare the two. What does this repetition tell us about the true author of their messages?

From the Commentary

The prophet Isaiah condemned Damascus, the capital of Syria (Isa. 17). Amos accused the Syrians of treating the people of Gilead like grain on a threshing floor (Amos 1:3–5). God would judge them for their inhumanity and brutality to His people.

According to Jeremiah, hearing the news of the approaching Babylonian army, the people of Damascus would become as troubled as the restless sea, as weak and shaky as a sick patient, and as full of pain as a woman in travail (Jer. 49:23–24). They would abandon their ancient cities and try to escape, but their best young men would be killed in the streets and their fortress would be burned to the ground.

—*Be Decisive*, page 194

5. The judgment against Syria (Jer. 49:23–27) is brief but powerful. What is the message here? What does this tell us about God's patience with sin? What does it teach us about God's consistency of character?

From the Commentary

As you studied these chapters, perhaps you became weary of reading the same message: Judgment is coming and there's no escape. There's a sameness about what God said about these nine nations, and if we aren't careful, that sameness can produce "tameness" and cause us to lose a heart sensitive to the Lord's message.

Keep in mind, however, that these prophecies were written about real men, women, and children, and that what Jeremiah wrote actually came true. Whole civilizations were wiped out because of their sins, and eventually Babylon itself was destroyed. This means that multitudes of people died and went into an eternity of darkness.

God sees what the nations do, and He rewards them justly.

God never gave the law of Moses to any of the nations that Jeremiah addressed, but He still held them accountable for the sins they committed against Him and against humanity. Because of the witness of creation around them and conscience within them, they were without excuse (Rom. 1:17–32, especially v. 20) and guilty before God.

—*Be Decisive*, pages 195–96

6. Read Isaiah 37:16; Joshua 3:11; Luke 10:21; and Acts 17:24. How do these verses speak to what was happening to the nations mentioned in Jeremiah? How did God hold these nations accountable for their actions? How does He do this with nations today?

From the Commentary

After declaring the destiny of the Gentile nations (Jer. 46—49), the prophet now focused on Judah's hateful enemy, the empire of Babylon. Jeremiah devoted 121 verses to the future of nine nations and 44 verses to the defeat and destruction of Jerusalem. When we count the number of verses in Jeremiah 50 and 51, however, he devoted 110 verses to the fall of Babylon. It is an important subject indeed!

In Scripture, the city of Babylon is contrasted with the city of Jerusalem—the proud city of man versus the Holy City of God. In Hebrew, the name *babel* means "gate of God," but *babel* is so close to the word *balal* ("confusion") that it's associated with the famous tower of Babel and the confusion of human languages (Gen. 11:1–9). The founder of Babylon was Nimrod (10:8–10), "a mighty hunter before the LORD" (v. 9). Some students interpret this to mean "a mighty rebel against the Lord." Babel/Babylon is a symbol of rebellion against God, the earthly city of human splendor opposing the heavenly city that glorifies God.

—*Be Decisive*, pages 199–200

7. What was the ultimate fate of Babylon? How did Babylon play a unique role in God's unfolding story? Why was it given so much attention in Jeremiah's prophecies?

More to Consider: There are many parallels between Jeremiah 50–51 and Revelation 17—18. Compare and contrast the two.

From the Commentary

"Announce and proclaim!" is the commandment in Jeremiah 50. "Raise the signal!" God declared war on Babylon and announced that her great god Bel (also called Marduk) was about to be shamefully defeated.

God declared war on both Babylon and the gods of Babylon. The word translated "idols" means "wooden blocks," and the word translated "images" means "dung pellets." The Lord didn't think much of their gods! The invaders would come from the north just as Nebuchadnezzar came from the north to conquer Judah (Jer. 1:11–15).

—*Be Decisive*, page 201

8. What does it mean that God "declared war on Babylon"? Why did Jeremiah use military language to describe its destruction? How would this sort of prophecy have been received by the people of God? By the Babylonian Empire?

Babylon that He was against them because of their pride (Jer. 50:31–32) and because of the way they had made the Jews suffer unnecessarily (v. 33). The exiles couldn't free themselves, but their strong Redeemer would free them! The phrase "plead their cause" speaks of a court case. Jehovah was defense attorney, judge, and jury, and He found Babylon guilty.

Now the Lord told Babylon what to expect on the day of their judgment. The first picture is that of a sword going through the land and cutting down the people (vv. 35–38). God's sword will even attack the waters and dry them up (v. 38). Why? Because it is "a land of idols" (v. 38 NIV), and God wanted to reveal that the idols were nothing. Like the overthrow of Sodom and Gomorrah, nothing will be left. Babylon will become a haven for animals and birds, and the city will never be restored.

The Lord directed the Babylonians' attention to the great army that He had called from the north—a cruel army without mercy, whose march sounded like "the roaring sea" (v. 42 NIV). This report paralyzed the king of Babylon. Like a hungry lion, looking for prey (see 49:19–21), Cyrus (and then Alexander) will attack Babylon, and nobody will be able to resist. God's chosen servant will always succeed. The Lord's judgment on Babylon will be like the winnowing of the grain: "Great Babylon" will be blown away like chaff along with its idols!

—*Be Decisive*, page 203

9. Summarize God's vivid message to the Babylonians. Why did God speak so strongly to this nation? How might the Jews (who were probably the ones who first heard this message) have responded to this prophecy? What do you think is a good response to make when we hear that God intends to pass judgment on other people?

From the Commentary

Throughout this prophecy, God has frequently announced the fall of Babylon, but the closing section seems to focus on God's total victory over the enemy.

God describes the victory in Jeremiah 51:27–33. God's armies were prepared, the commanders were ready, and the battle began; but the Babylonian army was helpless! They lay on the walls exhausted; their courage had failed them. The city was in flames, and the bars of the gates were broken. Nothing kept the enemy from entering the city and doing to it what the Babylonians had done to Jerusalem.

The Babylonians had an effective courier system and could quickly send messages to the various parts of their vast empire. In fact, Jeremiah described the runners meeting and exchanging messages for the king: "The river crossings have been seized!" "The marshes are set on fire!" "The soldiers are terrified!" "The city has been captured!" (see vv. 31–32 NIV). It was God's harvest, and Babylon was on the threshing floor.

God made it clear that there was no future in Babylon, for He had determined to destroy the city. If His people remained in Babylon, they would suffer the fate of the city. If they obeyed the Lord and returned home, they would experience a new beginning under the blessing of the Lord.

—*Be Decisive*, pages 205, 207

10. Why did God determine that Babylon had to be destroyed? (See Jer. 51:56.) What was God's message to the exiles held captive there? In what ways was He asking them to walk by faith and not by sight when He told them to leave the giant city? How is God's destruction of Babylon an example of His love for His people?

Looking Inward

Take a moment to reflect on all that you've explored thus far in this study of Jeremiah 46—51. Review your notes and answers and think about how each of these things matters in your life today.

Tips for Small Groups: To get the most out of this section, form pairs or trios and have group members take turns answering these questions. Be honest and as open as you can in this discussion, but most of all, be encouraging and supportive of others. Be sensitive to those who are going through particularly difficult times and don't press for people to speak if they're uncomfortable doing so.

11. Where do you see God's judgment today? How is the world after Jesus' life, death, and resurrection different from the world that went before? Have you ever felt judged like these many nations were? If so, how does your faith in Jesus answer that judgment?

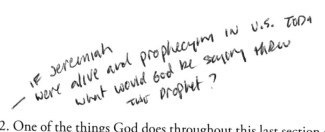
If Jeremiah were alive and prophecying in U.S. TODA what would God be saying thru this prophet?

12. <u>One of the things God does throughout this last section of Jeremiah is</u> <u>hold nations accountable for their actions.</u> If you were a nation, what would God be saying to you right now? How would God deliver that message to you? How would you respond to that message?

DANIEL WAS STILL LIVING IN BABYLON..
AND JEWS

13. The Israelites in captivity may have felt safe in Babylon's great city, but God told them they weren't. Have you ever felt like they did? What led to that false sense of security? In what ways is God asking you right now to "get out of Babylon"?   *Possible for us today ?*

Going Forward

14. Think of one or two things that you have learned that you'd like to work on in the coming week. Remember that this is all about quality, not quantity. It's better to work on one specific area of life and do it well than to work on many and do poorly (or to be so overwhelmed that you simply don't try).

Do you need to get out of Babylon? Be specific. Go back through Jeremiah 46—51 and put a star next to the phrase or verse that is most encouraging to you. Consider memorizing this verse.

Real-Life Application Ideas: Jeremiah is a book filled with history and a picture of God's reach across all nations. Take time this week to learn more about nations around the world. Soak up all you can about culture and religion in a few of these nations. Then spend time each evening praying for the leaders and people of each nation, asking God to reveal Himself to them and raise up leaders to spread the good news of God's love to them all.

Seeking Help

15. Write a prayer below (or simply pray one in silence), inviting God to work on your mind and heart in those areas you've noted in the Going Forward section. Be honest about your desires and fears.

Notes for Small Groups:

- *Look for ways to put into practice the things you wrote in the Going Forward section. Talk with other group members about your ideas and commit to being accountable to one another.*
- *During the coming week, ask the Holy Spirit to continue to reveal truth to you from what you've read and studied.*

Summary and Review

Notes for Small Groups: This session is a summary and review of this book. Because of that, it is shorter than the previous lessons. If you are using this in a small-group setting, consider combining this lesson with a time of fellowship or a shared meal.

Before you begin …
- *Pray for the Holy Spirit to reveal truth and wisdom as you go through this lesson.*
- *Briefly review the notes you made in the previous sessions. You will refer back to previous sections throughout this bonus lesson.*

Looking Back

1. Over the past eight lessons, you've examined the book of Jeremiah. What expectations did you bring to this study? In what ways were those expectations met?

2. What is the most significant personal discovery you've made from this study?

3. What surprised you most about the prophecies in Jeremiah? What, if anything, troubled you?

Progress Report

4. Take a few moments to review the Going Forward sections of the previous lessons. How would you rate your progress for each of the things you chose to work on? What adjustments, if any, do you need to make to continue on the path toward spiritual maturity?

5. In what ways have you grown closer to Christ during this study? Take a moment to celebrate those things. Then think of areas where you feel you still need to grow and note those here. Make plans to revisit this study in a few weeks to review your growing faith.

Things to Pray About

6. Jeremiah is a book about decisiveness—Jeremiah's decisiveness as a leader and God's decisiveness in judgment. As you reflect on the messages God gave Jeremiah to deliver, consider how decisiveness plays a role in your life and the world around you.

7. The messages in Jeremiah include judgment, trust, abuse of power, obedience, and, ultimately, hope. Spend time praying about each of these topics.

8. Whether you've been studying this in a small group or on your own, there are many other Christians working through the very same issues you discovered when examining the book of Jeremiah. Take time to pray for them, that God would reveal truth, that the Holy Spirit would guide you, and that each person might grow in spiritual maturity according to God's will.

A Blessing of Encouragement

Studying the Bible is one of the best ways to learn how to be more like Christ. Thanks for taking this step. In closing, let this blessing precede you and follow you into the next week while you continue to marinate in God's Word:

May God light your path to greater understanding as you review the truths found in the book of Jeremiah and consider how they can help you grow closer to Christ.